ADVANCE PRAISE

'A very insightful book on how to manage and counter-balance a new challenge to world-class brands: anti-brand activists and negative influencers in the age of social media. Dr Sood offers very practical strategies to shield your brands from negative attacks and fake news.'

Jagdish N. Sheth (Padma Bhushan),
Charles H. Kellstadt
Professor of Business, Goizueta Business School,
Emory University, Atlanta, GA, USA

'Branding has never been more fun to read! From fake news to brand hacktivism, the author cautions against these various weapons of brand destruction and provides strategies to counter your brand's doppelganger.'

Gagan Sood,
CEO, GE Power Conversion Americas,
GE, New York, USA

'This book is full of fun stories and examples of brand doppelganger imagery. The author shows how fake news and brand hacktivists can destroy your brand and provides strategies needed to counter the doppelgangers. A must-read for all branding professionals, students and pop culture followers.'

Atul Parvatiyar,
Director, Center for Sales and Customer Relationship
Excellence; Professor of Practice, Marketing and Supply
Chain Management, Rawls College of Business,
Texas Tech University, Lubbock, TX, USA

'Gaurav's passion is infectious, and the book has a compelling narrative on the brand of wicked doppelgangers who have an aim in sight to tarnish the image of brands. The author interestingly weaves the story around the evolution of doppelganger in the virtual world and his methodologies of carefully crafting negative imagery, creating attractive but damaging memes, trolling the brands exploiting their vulnerable spots and hacking their information to deliberately expose the negative sides of the brand. The doppelganger can be a harassed consumer, anti-brand activist, a clever competitor, an influencer or a media. The author plays with the fire of torching the brand of the companies through developing a brand alter ego, a doppelganger who can be a troll, hacktivist or an influencer. The topic is contemporary though having lots of grey and dark shades. Each page is generously scattered with carefully researched brand examples. Gaurav strategically establishes the factors leading to the creation of the brand doppelganger imagery, reassuringly emphasizes the art of storytelling and suggests counter strategies to combat and manage the menace of doppelgangers by bringing in the brand's positivity through knowing the pulse of their consumers and genuinely responding to their wants, needs and queries. The author has a razor-sharp insight and incisive analytic ability to bring to the fore the finer details of the uncanny world of the doppelganger, the brand alter ego, that makes this book one of the best branding's reference books around and a must-read for students, educators and industry professionals alike.'

Dr Amit Kapoor,
President and CEO, India Council on Competitiveness

'Dr Gaurav Sood has written an amazing book on branding which is much needed by the industry and academics. The entire branding paradigm has changed as there are drastic changes among the consumers, companies, competitors, media and society. This change is wonderfully narrated in the book. Must-read for all the marketing and business professionals.'

Professor Varsha Jain,
Marketing; Co-chairperson, Doctoral Programme and Research, MICA, Ahmedabad, Gujarat, India

'A must-read book for branding enthusiasts and pop culture followers.'

Professor Sandeep Puri,
Asian Institute of Management, Manila, Philippines

'This book has some very interesting insights on important issues such as brand doppelganger imagery, culture jamming, fake news and internet trolls that many brands face today.'

Dr Sunil Thomas,
Professor, California State University, Fullerton, CA, USA

'This book is a storyteller! It weaves real cases from the world of branding to explore the phenomenon of brand doppelganger imagery.'

Sumit Sehgal,
Director, Samsung SDS

'A must-read for all digital marketers as this book analyses various forms of online consumer backlash and how consumers, competition and public at large create a brand doppelganger imagery using the social media platforms to damage the brand's imagery.'

Amitabh Verma,
Ex-Google; Founder and CEO, AMP Digital

'The concept of brand doppelganger has been very fascinatingly brought up by Dr Sood and his breadth of experience in industry and academia has lent weight to his insights and theories on the subject. Media landscape, both offline and online, is haunted by fake news, trolls and consumer backlashes which make the big brands vulnerable to the creation of their own doppelganger.'

Rajiv Dubey,
Senior General Manager and
Head of Media, Dabur

'Most books on branding make few connections to the current brand management environment. This book written by Dr Gaurav Sood is designed explicitly for the new world of brand and branding. A blend of theory and practice, with cases from the global brands, the book brings alive the critical dimensions of 'brand doppel-ganger' in a crisp yet comprehensive manner.'

Hari Krishnan,
Strategic Advisor, Culture Drum

'A truly International brand playbook. Gaurav's argu-ments are thorough and persuasive and his breath of academic and professional experience all across the globe has helped to reflect in his story telling. The book *Troll Proof Branding in the Age of Doppelgangers* take aim at the darker side of the brand and the impact of the brand doppelgänger on the reputation of the brand. The book is an eye-opening reportage and wonderful analysis of how trolls, fake news, hacktivism and culture jamming creates brand's own doppelganger and threatens its image in the popular culture. Gaurav has carefully anal-ysed cases from across the world of brands which are victim to its own doppelganger. The book is a must-read for marketers and students to learn how to develop counter strategies and manage the brand doppelganger.'

Douglas Quintal,
Sr Executive-in-Residence, Emerson College,
Boston, MA, USA

TROLL PROOF
BRANDING
in the Age of
DOPPELGANGERS

SAGE Response, our business books imprint, celebrates its silver jubilee this year. As we reflect on this transformational journey that began with a single title, we thank everyone who has helped us to produce content that is topical and relevant across a varied audience of aspiring managers, working professionals, practitioners and students. We feel privileged that eminent management and leadership experts, professionals and stalwarts from academia supported and trusted us with their work. Over the years, SAGE Response has built an enviable list of practice-based, reader-friendly books that provide creative strategies to keep pace with the rapidly changing global scenario. As we grow and evolve with the times, it is our endeavour to continue to publish books that offer innovative solutions, approaches and perspectives to the disciplines that we serve.

TROLL PROOF
BRANDING
in the Age of
DOPPELGANGERS

GAURAV SOOD

Los Angeles | London | New Delhi
Singapore | Washington DC | Melbourne

First published in 2022 by

SAGE Publications India Pvt Ltd
B1/I-1 Mohan Cooperative Industrial Area
Mathura Road, New Delhi 110 044, India
www.sagepub.in

SAGE Publications Inc
2455 Teller Road
Thousand Oaks, California 91320, USA

SAGE Publications Ltd
1 Oliver's Yard, 55 City Road
London EC1Y 1SP, United Kingdom

SAGE Publications Asia-Pacific Pte Ltd
18 Cross Street #10-10/11/12
China Square Central
Singapore 048423

Published by Vivek Mehra for SAGE Publications India Pvt Ltd. Typeset in 11/14pt ITC Stone Serif by Fidus Design Pvt Ltd, Chandigarh.

Library of Congress Control Number: 2021951370

ISBN: 978-93-5479-353-0 (PB)

SAGE Team: Namarita Kathait, Neena Ganjoo and Rajinder Kaur

To my wife, Manpreet,
and my son, Rohan

Thank you for choosing a SAGE product!
If you have any comment, observation or feedback,
I would like to personally hear from you.

Please write to me at **contactceo@sagepub.in**

Vivek Mehra, Managing Director and CEO, SAGE India.

CONTENTS

LIST OF ABBREVIATIONS

AI   : Artificial intelligence

BCG : Boston Consulting Group

BCM : Brand concept mapping

BJP   : Bharatiya Janata Party

BOGO : Buy one get one

C2C   : Consumer-to-consumer

CES   : Consumer Electronics Show

CII   : Confederation of Indian Industry

DDoS : Distributed denial of service

DEC   : Delhi Election Commission

EPL   : English Premier League

FBI   : Federal Bureau of Investigation

FDA   : Food and Drug Administration

FMCG : Fast-moving consumer goods

GCPL : Godrej Consumer Products Limited

GS&P : Goodby, Silverstein & Partners

HTA   : Hindustan Thompson Associates

IE   : Internet Explorer

IMC   : Integrated marketing communication

INC   : Indian National Congress

IPC   : Indian Penal code

IPL   : Indian Premier League

ISIL	:	Islamic State of Iraq and the Levant
ISIS	:	Islamic State of Iraq and Syria
IVR	:	Interactive voice response
JNU	:	Jawaharlal Nehru University
JWT	:	J. Walter Thompson
NBA	:	National Basketball Association
NBL	:	National Basketball League
NFL	:	National Football League
NLP	:	Natural language processing
NPR	:	National Population Register
NRC	:	National Register of Citizens
O&M	:	Ogilvy & Mather
OTC	:	Over-the-counter
OTT	:	Over-the-top
PC	:	Personal computer
PM	:	Prime Minister
PR	:	Public relation
RJ	:	Radio jockey
TAG	:	Threat Analysis Group
TRPs	:	TV rating points
TV	:	Television
UEFA	:	Union of European Football Associations
UGC	:	User-generated content
USP	:	Unique selling proposition
VFX	:	Visual effects
XSS	:	Cross-site scripting
ZMET	:	Zaltman's metaphor elicitation technique

Troll Proof Branding in the Age of Doppelgangers

FOREWORD

It was a cold winter evening in December 2003. I was busy organizing the exchange4media advertising conference at Hotel Hyatt Regency where I met Dr Gaurav Sood. Gaurav had completed his third master's degree from Boston, USA, and was then working in the corporate sector in a global organization and was or I may say is a successful marketing and advertising professional. His professional engagements have made him travel across the world, particularly the Americas and Germany. He observes, listens and processes, and it is a delight to listen to him. We discussed ideas around marketing, media and advertising towards building a specific industry community. He wanted to write articles for exchange4media and later on contributed many articles in the *BW Businessworld* magazine. He is an avid scribbler on brand and advertising. Over the years, Dr Sood completed his doctorate degree and moved into academia where his love for writing and observing marketing trends and distilling the future got further honed.

Gaurav, in the last two plus decades of working, has lived a life as a corporate leader, a community builder, an author, an academician and an observer of business trends. He has a global perceptive which he gained from his educational background and industry experience working with varied brands and consumer cultures. I myself have watched closely the changing paradigms in global businesses and how digital technologies have changed the way we do business and build brands. Both Gaurav and I have lived life in a suitcase, bumping each other at airports and working while waiting for connecting flights. We all work towards developing and growing ourselves and the way Gaurav has planned his transition from corporate to academia is commendable. Gaurav is never satisfied by learning about one side of the coin, and he believes in flipping and studying the other side too. This remark is an acceptance to how he looks at the positive and the negative side of a brand ecosystem and how he can help the marketers through this book to develop counter strategies to fight their own doppelganger.

The COVID-19 pandemic has accelerated the digital economy. Brands as well as businesses are built digitally. The book deals with the issues of fake news, hacktivism, internet trolls and culture jamming and dissects them as rampant pop culture phenomena in the age of consumerism. D2C, known as digital to consumer or direct to consumer, is the reality of this digital age and economy. In this economy, a brand's image is fragile to a competitor's tactics, the very aware consumer and the need to win the race to become the market leader. All that a competitor or a miffed unsatisfied consumer needs to do to bring down a brand's image is to go online and spread the message mocking the brand. The stronger a brand, the more vulnerable it is to the creation of its own doppelganger. The book establishes the fact that brands have been threatened by its their doppelgangers and if not dealt with, then they can damage the reputation of the brand. The book discusses many such cases, Starbucks, Nike, Narendra Modi, Rahul Gandhi, Indian Premier League, United Airlines, Botox, etc., which have been haunted by their own doppelgangers. How can branding become more positive? Despite backlashes, how can organizations ensure they keep their customers satisfied and the brand doppelganger locked away?

Troll Proof Branding in the Age of Doppelgangers mulls over these questions and courageously tackles them through various case studies and counter strategies.

Gaurav deserves kudos for articulating a playbook or brand reference book for building brands in a D2C economy. Read this book to know how brands can build and safeguard their brand reputation in the age of brand doppelgangers.

Annurag Batra,
Chairman and Editor-in-Chief, BW Businessworld
Media Group and Exchange4media Media Group

PREFACE

This was the summer of 2012, and after a successful career in marketing working all across the globe, I was looking for some avenues to share my experience with management students, probably in the form of a guest faculty. I went to meet the director of my alma mater (IMT, Ghaziabad) and asked him for such an opportunity. He then referred me to another B-School which had a tie-up with Lancaster University in India. After initial interaction, the management offered me a faculty position, and that's how I became an 'accidental professor' and came into academics. Soon I realized that the corporate experience and my three master's degrees were not good enough to grow in academics. So I started preparing for my PhD research and started looking for a research topic. I wanted to research the 'place branding', but after the literature review I found that it was done to death and the scope was also limited. So leaving my comfort zone, I started looking for a topic which had not been widely researched and came across a research paper by a Lancaster University, UK, faculty on 'Revenge of the Brand Monsters: How Goldman Sachs' Doppelgänger Turned Monstrous'. The word 'doppelganger' fascinated me, and I dived deep into understanding the history of the word and its relationship with brand and its imagery. For one year I researched and studied brand and its negative imagery created by its stakeholders, competition, media and public at large. Since Indian Premier League (IPL) was mired in controversies around match-fixing, black money, spot-fixing, glamour, etc., I decided to choose the IPL brand for my PhD research area and empirically analysed the impact of the brand doppelganger imagery on IPL. I used the brand concept mapping technique to construct the network of brand associations of IPL and then statistically analysed the impact. To my utter surprise, despite a strong brand doppelganger, IPL's brand value was still on the up and the impact of the monstrous IPL's brand doppelganger had no negative impact on its brand imagery, but somehow the controversies and negative associations helped the brand.

This made me further study other brands and their doppelganger imagery and how these brands have responded to it. After writing few articles which stemmed out of my research in leading business magazines and publishing a book on *Impact of Doppelgänger Brand Image on Indian Premiere League (IPL)*, I was keen to publish the phenomenon of brand doppelganger to make the marketers and management students aware of the concept and how it is created and managed by different brands across the globe.

To understand the phenomenon of 'doppelganger', I had to go back to the book written by Robert Louis Stevenson in 1927 *The Strange Case of Dr. Jekyll & Mr. Hyde*. This classic by Stevenson explores the dual personality of Dr Jekyll, whose darker side is Mr Hyde, who is evil and monstrous rendition of the otherwise good guy Dr Jekyll. Every human has an alter ego like Dr Jekyll, and it is exactly opposite to the personality of that person, for example, Superman is the alter ego of Clark Kent. This whole idea of two personality nature has become a part of the popular culture, becoming synonymous with dual personalities as a reflection of the same coin, one good and one bad.

Doppelganger brand image, by definition, is a collection of disapproving images and stories about a brand which are circulated in popular culture by a fairly loosely organized network of anti-brand activists, bloggers, opinion leaders and consumers. The word 'doppelganger' comes from the German vocabulary, where *doppel* means double and *ganger* means walker. Thus, a doppelganger is a double walker. The basis of this is that individuals have altered ego and that is negative, evil and monstrous mirror effect of the spirit of the individual. So how is this relevant to brands? Brands try to create a positive image in the minds of their consumers through various marketing and branding strategies. They want consumers to think positively about them and to have strong, favourable and unique associations with them. The brands which have strong associations develop a favourable influence on consumers' intention to buy. But I figured out after researching many top brands that all was not well with them, and the stronger the brand, the more vulnerable it becomes to the cultural backlash, known as 'brand doppelganger image'.

This book analyses various forms of consumer backlash and anti-brand activism and how culture jamming, fake news, trolling and hacktivism create the brand doppelganger imagery and try to destroy the cultural ideology and reputation of the brand both offline and online. It also suggests the empirical measurement of the brand doppelganger and how the monstrous image can be managed by marketers and brand managers.

I hope that the book will be relevant to the management students and marketers to get an insight as to how the brand doppelganger imagery can be created, measured and managed by learning through various instances and case studies of top global brands.

ACKNOWLEDGEMENTS

First of all, I would like to thank my publisher SAGE, editor Namarita Kathait and Manisha Mathews for having faith in me and continuously guiding me and running after me to complete the book. I'd also like to thank the people who have helped me learn and practise both the art and science of branding throughout the years.

A special thanks is due to Professor (Dr) J. K. Sharma, my PhD supervisor, for inspiring me to research and write books and to my friends Sandeep Mann and K. M. Tripathi for catching my fall and supporting my flight. I would also like to thank all my colleagues who have been part of my career at one point or the other and have believed in me till now.

An additional thanks is due to all the organizations who have given me an opportunity to learn and work for them and to Amity University, where I am able to further continue my teaching, research and especially learning the many facets of the process of building an academic leader.

I'd also like to thank all those people who have shaped my life personally and given me unconditional support, including my parents, wife, son, brother and relatives and friends.

CHAPTER 1

THE MONSTER UNLEASHED

In India, Cricket is believed to be not just a sporting event but a religious practice. We saw a new wave of change with the Britishers introducing Cricket to India in the early 1700, and since then the sport has become a nationwide addiction. The sport was coined as the 'gentlemen's game' because of the rules introduced by the Britishers which shunned sledging, cheating and bodyline bowling as unethical. That was the scenario then, and what we see today is a complete gruesome makeover of the sport. The scenario which changed with time demanded a crispy and short version, and there the birth of 20-20 cricket league took place. Cricket became a source of a new kind of entertainment with the pompous launch of the Indian Premier League (IPL) in 2007, a format which involved auctioning of players, bidding, franchise, hiring international cheerleaders and tons of money laundering.[1] Inside IPL, promoters, franchise owners and players are running an extravagant business, which has become the centre of attraction. The betting in the game leads to match-fixing, which has derogated the position of cricket which was once known as a

---

[1] https://www.thehindubusinessline.com/news/sports/ipl-money laundering-case-ed-seeks-aid-from-singapore-mauritius/article 7370065.ece

gentlemen sport. IPL allows Indian fans above 18 years of age to bet by simply opening an account at a bookmaker using a betting license.[2]

Cricket is a game of uncertainty, as you cannot predict what is going to happen on the next ball. Will the player hit it for a six or will he be out? Speculations as to what will happen next soar high, and the business of betting grows many folds. In fact, betting isn't just limited to putting your money on what you think will happen next. Heavy betting and huge investments made on players breed spot or match-fixing, which leads to many players underperform to gain monetary benefits. Soon, a dark shadowy image of IPL came into existence, the one which is marred with controversies. Where Sreesanth controversy was a slap gate, another news of Harbhajan and Sreesanth rocked the nation. Besides these, IPL has also been associated with series of controversies such as sacking of its chairman Lalit Modi for misconduct and financial irregularities, Pakistani players being officially banned from coming to India post the Mumbai attack and a threatening act between Kings XI Punjab franchise owners Preity Zinta and Ness Wadia.[3]

As this ugly side of IPL surfaced, it created many media debates and fan backlashes and put a black spot on the once-famous league and to the gentlemen game. Fans started expressing their disappointment on social media by sharing disparaging images and memes and trolling the players. Media experts announced doom for IPL and appealed to close down the league, as it brought a bad

[2] https://www.hindustantimes.com/cities/pune-news/ipl-betting-two-arrested-rs-93-lakh-seized-by-pune-police-101632766309321.html https://blog.ipleaders.in/case-study-of-the-ipl-spot-fixing-and-betting-case/

[3] https://www.freepressjournal.in/sports/cricket/ipl-controversies-preity-zinta-and-ness-wadia

reputation to the sport. IPL brand was beaten and bruised by anti-fans and soon emerged as a gruesome evil twin, destroying the once loved and worshipped game. The circulation of disparaging images and stories by IPL fans in the popular media led to the creation of a strong monstrous IPL doppelganger imagery.

'Everything can be branded which includes people, place, things, festivals, etc. People as a brand sometimes are more important than the Company itself,' says Kevin Lane Keller, a professor and the author of *Strategic Brand Management.*

Steve Jobs, Richard Branson, Baba Ramdev, M. S. Dhoni, Amitabh Bachchan, Virat Kohli and many other personalities as themselves are known to be powerful brands. Their image and brand value are as valuable as any product or brand attached to them. These 'personal brands' can sell products, but sometimes the brands that celebrities sell come under scrutiny for their ill practices or malicious hidden intentions. It also happens that an image which is contrary to the one that the personal brand stands for surfaces. Such negative images of brands are harmful and challenge the core positive brand associations and eventually create a narrative opposite to the brand's proposition to the consumers. As said by Jeff Bezos, the founder of Amazon, 'Your brand is what people say about you when you're not in the room.'

In the 21st century, politicians also hold the same brand power as media stars because of their extensive use of social media, particularly Twitter, to communicate their messages, which are even more influential than the mainstream media. Political leaders such as 44th US President Barack Obama with 129 million Twitter followers and Indian Prime Minister (PM) Narender Modi with above 65 million followers are powerful personal brands. Rahul Gandhi, the current leader of India's oldest party, Congress, has around 17 million Twitter followers. Social media does help politicians to stay active with current matters where they regularly tweet their opinions, ideologies and reactions to various topical issues of the nation. At the same time, social media acts as a double-edged sword which can make and break images.

Let's analyse the situation Rahul Gandhi got himself into. During the run-up of the 2014 general elections, Amit Shah referred Rahul Gandhi as 'Pappu'[4] in his quote,

> The Congress thinks the Prime Minister's chair is Pappu's birthright. But this is a democracy, you need people's blessings, and people's blessings are with Narendra Modi. We have declared our PM candidate (Narendra Modi). Who will be the Congress candidate? Pappu? No, they won't make Pappu their candidate as they are afraid of losing.

With this quote, social media blasted with 'Pappu' jokes, undermining Rahul Gandhi's credibility, which was a win for the opposition.

Since that day, 'Pappu' is still a catchphrase synonymous with Rahul Gandhi. 'Pappu' imagery has permanently stuck to Rahul Gandhi since April 2013, when he went to address a conference at the Confederation of Indian Industry (CII). The top trending Twitter hashtag on that day was #PappuCII. The birth of the name 'Pappu' was further popularized by remembering the Bollywood song 'Pappu Can't Dance Sala' and not to forget the famous Amitabh Bachchan advertisement of Cadbury Dairy Milk chocolate 'Pappu Pass Ho Gaya'. Passing an exam is a moment of celebration, but when the local stupid and

Troll Proof Branding in the Age of Doppelgangers

----

[4] 'Pappu' generally in India refers to someone innocent and dumb, one who is not worldly wise and is an underdog, who does not stand a chance to win.

slow learner does it, it calls for an even sweeter celebration and that's what the Cadbury advertisement does by extending its core positioning of 'celebrating happiness' with the brand mantra 'Kuchh Meetha Ho Jaye'. In 2008, Delhi Election Commission (DEC) ran a campaign 'Pappu Can't Vote', which basically was targeted at people who decide not to vote and for whom being part of the electoral process is not important. Carrying on with this imagery and constantly being attacked and referred to as 'Pappu', Rahul Gandhi and his party were defeated in the general elections and were reduced to merely 44 Parliament seats. Although this may not be the sole reason for the defeat, however, it plays some role in tarnishing the prince of Congress party's imagery in the public.

Although Rahul Gandhi has covered a distance from 'Pappu' to 'popular', he has paid the price of his monstrous imagery created in the popular culture.

In the above two instances, we see the emergence of a negative phenomenon. It is not something that hasn't been caught by the media, marketers or brand researchers before; however, in this book, we will be discussing this phenomenon with a far thorough lens. So let's understand the brand doppelganger imagery concept and why brands and their organizations need to carefully monitor and manage it.

To understand the phenomenon of 'doppelganger', we need to go back to the book written by Robert Louis Stevenson in 1927 *The Strange Case of Dr. Jekyll & Mr. Hyde*. This classic by Stevenson explores the dual personality of Dr Jekyll, whose darker side Mr Hyde, who is an evil and monstrous rendition of the otherwise good guy Dr Jekyll. This concept isn't too far from reality. In psychology, the existence of an alter ego is well documented. Alter egos like Dr Jekyll are aspects of a person which exist metaphorically. It is exactly opposite to the personality of that person. Pop culture has exemplified it well through Superman, whose alter ego is Clark Kent. These dual personalities are a reflection of the same coin, existing as good and bad together.

We can define doppelganger brand image as a collection of disapproving images and stories about a brand which are circulated in popular culture by a fairly loosely organized network of anti-brand activists, bloggers, opinion leaders and consumers. The word 'doppelganger' comes from the German vocabulary, where *doppel* means double and *ganger* means walker. Thus, a doppelganger is a double walker. It was based upon the notion that humans possess an alter ego which is negative, evil and a monstrous reflection of an individual.

Todd Herman in his book *The Alter Ego Effect* explained that we need to unlock our alter ego to discover the hero within us. Todd revealed the secrets of many performing athletes and executives. Using the story of Bo Jackson, a former Baseball and Football star, he established his theory of the alter ego effect. He cited how Bo Jackson unlocked his alter ego after watching *Friday the 13th* movie and used Jason's, the movie character, cold and calculative personality on the field and channelized his anger as a winning strategy. But sometimes you may discover the darker side, the immoral side, of yours too. This was very well reflected in the movie *Spider-Man 3*, where one day, an alien symbiote attached itself to Peter's Spider-Man suit and turned it black. This black suit gave immense power to the Spider-Man and turned him into a venomous Spider-Man—known as Venom. The black suit took control of Peter by giving him more power and brought out the darker side of his personality—his alter ego. Later in the movie, Peter struggled to reach into his deep inner self to gain strength to fight the sinfulness inflicted on him by the alien symbiote.

SO HOW IS THIS RELEVANT TO BRANDS?

Brands try to create a positive image in the minds of their consumers through various marketing and branding strategies. They want consumers to think positively about them and have strong, favourable and unique associations with them. The brands which have strong associations develop a favourable influence on consumers' intention to buy. Apple tops the chart with a brand value of around $263 billion in 2021.[5] Associations of words used such as 'design', 'creative' and 'innovation' are ingrained into the core brand value of Apple. Consumers buy into these associations every year when Apple launches its new phone or products. Starbucks, the biggest name in the coffee shop retail industry with a brand value of over $11.5 billion, was a humble effort by three academicians from Seattle, Washington, USA. Their love for coffee made it possible to open Starbucks, a name inspired by the character in the classic novel

[5] https://www.statista.com/statistics/264875/brand-value-of-the-25-most-valuable-brands/

Moby-Dick. In 1981 , a salesman named Howard Schultz selling drip coffee makers was so impressed by Starbucks that he joined it as a marketing head and deviated the business from a coffee and equipment seller to the idea of converting it into a coffeehouse chain serving espressos and cappuccinos and later food items too. Schultz once quoted in an interview to NBC,

> You can create shareholder value and you can create value for your people. We've also learned something at Starbucks that by doing good things to your people, your customers are going to build a large reservoir of trust around the equity of the brand because they want to support a company whose values are compatible with their own.[6]

But all that glitter is not gold. Starbucks was also vulnerable, as brand messages are managed not only by the brand managers and CEO but also by user interactions through word of mouth and user-generated content (UGC).

EMOTIONAL BRANDING STRATEGY IS NOT ENOUGH!

The stronger the brand, the more vulnerable it becomes to the cultural backlash, known as 'brand doppelganger image'. Starbucks brought a spike in coffee consumption in America and the world over and became an important cultural representation. No doubt, Starbucks had a strong emotional connect with its stakeholders and has been able to position successfully in the minds of the consumers, but emotional branding strategies have their lacuna, as benefit-driven positioning strategies may sometimes backfire too. Not everyone is happy with others' success, and even a rapidly expanding and successful brand like Starbucks can raise some eyebrows. With corporate cafes

[6] https://www.cnbc.com/2019/03/11/howard-schultz-on-the-starbucks-brand-i-know-a-little-about-marketing.html

taking over and mom-and-pop coffee shops running out of business, Starbucks became the target of anti-Starbucks activists because of the negative impact of the fast and pompous growth of the coffee leader. It was perceived that Starbucks was responsible for crushing the local competition by making mom-and-pop stores run out of business in America. To gain market leadership, Starbucks has over the years adopted many strategies such as buying leases of the competition, opening many outlets in one geographical location and internationally operating at loss. They were also involved in labour disputes, over-pricing their products and serving less coffee to reduce milk cost. Such decisions embroiled Starbucks in many controversies, which damaged its reputation and gave further reasons for the anti-Starbucks lobby to attack the brand.

Emotional branding strategies like other marketing strategies are not foolproof to consumer backlash. These backlashes can parody the brand positioning and degrade the core positioning on which the brand has achieved its competitive advantage. Starbucks is not the only brand facing consumer backlash. The list is long and includes many super brands such as Apple, Microsoft and Nike. For example, Nike was accused of running sweatshops, Apple received government and consumer backlash on deliberately slowing down older iPhones and Microsoft was accused of unfair monopolistic practices. Starbucks has many positive brand catchphrases such as *sophisticated, relaxing, comfortable, fresh* and *exotic* but it has also garnered many negative associations such as *superior, pretentious, confusing* and *expensive*. This shows that consumers are no longer inactive participants in brand building; rather, they are actively involved in its success or failure. Not only do the consumers give constructive feedback to the brands, but they also communicate among themselves and form an impact on the very existence of the consumer-to-consumer (C2C) marketing/branding. These brand communities include the shared brand owners and can contribute to the development of a brand from product design, usage and innovation and can even be the spokesperson in brand advertising. Harley Davidson brand communities are a real example of shared brand ownership. But they can also sometimes culture jam brand communication, especially when they find that the brand essence is getting diluted and the brand is breaking its promise. Consumers, anti-brand activists and other stakeholders may put a spammer in the brand wheel and create a brand doppelganger image by circulating negative comments, reviews, memes, etc., through blogs and social media platforms.

Starbucks brand doppelganger image could best be understood from a Starbucks haters' website 'We Hate Starbucks',[7] which states

> WE HATE STARBUCKS! Home Sweet Starbucks! Starbucks, that nice place to have a coffee, with its arty, eco friendly, homely appeal. It makes you feel all special, like your some kind of flaneur, a real person of the new millennium, stopping your busy lifestyle to break for coffee. Starbucks is your thing, you feel like a Sartre or some other French intellectual. You my friend are a Mug.... Their attempts at portraying a modern arty cafe culture, with left leanings are just a caked on makeup, for the neoliberal global capitalist thug that they are. Destroying land with their farming methods and lives with their wages to farmers and workers alike.

Well, there are Starbucks lovers too, as not all consumers will be lobbying against the brand. However, sometimes even media jumps the bandwagon. Onion is an American satirical digital media company and *newspaper* organizations. Their headline reads 'New Starbucks Opens in Rest

[7] https://www2.spacehijackers.org/starbucks/

Room of Existing Starbucks'.[8] Where further mocking of the brand in social media damaged the coffee leader image, the Starbucks fans were also mocked to be snooty and trend followers.

Media can also play its role in tarnishing the image of a brand by contradicting the brand message through their anchors, spokespersons, debates and talk shows. We see many news channels taking sides on a particular issue, whether about political party or celebrity personality. Martha Stewart is one such example. She got engulfed in a series of scandals, false narratives and culture satires. All this led to serious issues for the Martha Stewart brand management exercise.[9] Nike also faced such flanks and was accused of running sweatshops in the 1990s in China, Taiwan and South Korea.[10] Media accused them of outsourcing their production to factories which employed manual labour at very low wages, for long hours, and work in poor conditions. Most of the anti-sweatshop groups were led by students and mainly women in their teens or early 20s. Nike's director's statement, 'Hey, we don't own the factories. We don't control what goes on there,' did not do any good, and Nike was criticized all over the world, which shaped the an anti-brand campaign 'Just Don't Do It' to boycott the use of Nike products. Nike came to face its horrifying doppelganger. To tackle it, it installed a code of conduct called SHAPE—safety, health, attitude, people and environment—in the factories of the countries in question.

---

[8] https://www.theonion.com/new-starbucks-opens-in-rest-room-of-existing-starbucks-1819564800.

[9] https://danielsethics.mgt.unm.edu/pdf/martha%20stewart%20case.pdf

[10] https://www.thefashionlaw.com/visibility-is-central-to-a-successful-supply-chain-heres-what-brands-need-to-know/

The anti-brand activists who could be anyone from consumer to media hijack the brand proposition and create a monstrous image of the brand which can tarnish its reputation leading to brand avoidance and a drop in revenue and profits. Such anti-brand actions are in the form of playing with the brand logo, twisting the brand tagline, demeaning the brand proposition and making it look atrocious. Consumers, competitions, anti-brand activists and public at large can today use social media to express their discontent on failed brand promises and take further retaliation. What happened with Tiger Woods, regarded as one of the greatest golfers of all times, a gentleman athlete and a sporting phenomenon to a disgraced sporting celebrity? It all started with the crash of his SUV, and what happened next was breaking news and public and media attraction. In the early morning of 27 November 2009, Tiger Woods crashed his SUV in his neighbour's backyard, which created a big sound waking up his wife. She, with the help of the golf club, broke the SUV window and took him out. Tiger was fined $164 for careless driving. Media scented the blood and descended on the scene exposing the golfer's hidden affair with other women. This was established when the media discovered a voicemail message in Tiger's voice on the phone of Jaimee Grubbs, a 24-year-old waitress who claimed to be the object of golfer Tiger Woods's alleged extramarital likings.

Tiger had to admit and made the statement,

> I was unfaithful, I had affairs and I cheated. What I did was unacceptable, I hurt my wife, my kids, my mother, my wife's family, my friends, my foundation, and kids all around the world who admired me. I knew my actions were wrong but I convinced myself that normal rules didn't apply. I never thought about who I was hurting, instead, I thought only about myself, I ran straight through

the boundaries a married couple should live by. I thought I could get away with whatever I wanted to. I felt that I had worked hard my entire life and deserved to enjoy all the temptations around me. I felt I was entitled, and thanks to money and fame, I didn't have to go far to find them.[11]

But the damage to his image was done! Tiger took a sabbatical from golf to work on his image. Brands such as Accenture, AT&T, Gatorade and General Motors pulled back their sponsorships, except Nike.

Social media, particularly Twitter, was leading in the share of voice, where 80 per cent of the tweets were responding to the Tiger scandal in media. Comments like 'By cheating on his wife, especially in such a disgusting and complete way, Tiger has utterly spoiled the last sport that had generally been considered a sport of gentlemen (and gentlewomen, of course). After all, cheaters are cheaters' were circulating. Jokes on him started circulating on social media: 'Tiger Woods is the first person in history to run his car into a hydrant and set himself on fire.' Many polls were run on Twitter where he got negative votes. Woods's voice email to one of his affairs requesting to delete his messages was publicized by Twitterati through a video,[12] generating 90 per cent negative comments. Brands associated with Tiger—Gatorade and Nike—became part of the joke. Twitterati conversations used the brands' slogans 'Just Do It' (Nike) and 'Is It in You?' (Gatorade) to make jokes about the story. A strong monstrous doppelganger brand image emerged, leading to the fall of Tiger Woods.

[11] https://www.ndtv.com/sports-news/full-transcript-of-tiger-woodss-statement-411303

[12] https://www.youtube.com/watch?v=OEkomaBTppY

I call this doppelganger imagery the brand monster. This doppelganger imagery is a brand image created by the stakeholders to expose the hidden wickedness of the brand. It attacks the brands which do not employ an effective emotional or cultural brand strategy, whereas sometimes these strategies can be more vulnerable to the formation of a brand monster. When anthropomorphized doppelganger images are attached to a brand in question, a dark metaphorical image is formed in the minds of consumers. This makes the brand vulnerable and an easy target to attack effectively.

Brand anthropomorphism is herein defined as the extent to which a branded product is perceived as an actual human being. Marketers define the personality of a brand with human characteristics and want consumers to personify brands. Brand personality is defined as 'a set of human personality traits ascribed to a brand'.[13] Sometimes the marketers anthropomorphize their brands with some mascot or human representation such as Pillsbury Doughboy, Tony the Tiger and Vodafone ZooZoo. Anthropomorphizing helps people understand brands and make more sense of what kind of role they can play in their lives. Also, it defines the relationship that a person will have with their brand; for example, many people consider mobile phones and cars as their companions. There could be three forms of anthropomorphism. First, when people consider some of the traits of a brand as a human; for example, they see a face as the front of a car. Second, they by mistake consider an object or animal is a person; for example, they may mistake a trash bag lying on the roadside to be a sitting person. Finally, when people imagine that there are some human

---

[13] https://howbrandsarebuilt.com/blog/2018/11/01/definition-what-is-brand-personality/

elements in objects like a face on the mountain.[14] Products and brands have also been perceived to have human-like characteristics; for example, people talk to their motorbikes as a friend and children talk to their barbie dolls or toys as they perceive them to be their friends and even carry them to sleep for warmth and security.

Brand monsters create a negative image about a brand by using the tactic of anthropomorphizing the brand into something opposite. Sometimes, this can even help expose the gap between brand promise and actual performance. The brand monster can help shed light on a brand's hidden agendas by creative imagery and illustration. Capitalism, a popular concept, was unravelled as a bloodsucking vampire, sucking the blood and tears of the labour class by Karl Marx. This imagery helped in spreading awareness about the negative effects of capitalism. Similarly, financial markets are many times blamed for their irregularities and lack of transparency. We have seen what happened to the multinational investment bank and financial services company, Goldman Sachs, a USA-based financial institution. It was deemed as the foremost representative of capitalism and soon got associated with a bloodsucking vampire imagery. *Rolling Stone,* an American monthly magazine which emphasizes popular culture, defined Goldman Sachs as a 'great vampire squid', who was responsible for sucking money and orchestrating all the financial market manipulations since the worldwide economic depression in the 1930s. When the mortgage market collapsed in 2007–2008, Goldman Sachs was responsible for misleading its investors and made a profit from the financial

[14] P. Aggarwal and A. L. McGill, 'Is That Car Smiling at Me? Schema Congruity as a Basis for Evaluating Anthropomorphized Products', *Journal of Consumer Research* 34, no. 4 (2007): 468–479.

market crash.[15] Although initially Goldman Sachs denied the allegations, later it admitted to the fraud and paid $550 million as settlement. Acting as an invisible entity to its investors, Goldman Sachs represented the cold image of the banking industry which was considered to be remote, complex and inscrutable. Some of the Wall Street imagery as a greedy and heartless place was developed by Jordan Belfort, better known as 'Wolf on the Wall Street'.[16] Belfort was accused of financial market frauds of money laundering and security frauds. He was accused of manipulating the penny stock market by practising 'pump and dump' trading scheme. This manipulative scheme worked through brokers who were employed by Belfort, and these brokers used misleading information about companies and their stocks to the public and sold the lower-priced stocks to them and then later sold Belfort and its team stocks to make the share of the company collapse in the stock market and make money out of it at the cost of losses to the investors. Both Goldman Sachs and Jordan Belfort acted as vampires and sucked the blood of their investors by manipulating the stock market and cheating the investors. This led to the creation of their 'blood sucker vampire' doppelganger imagery and led to their collapse. How this vampire squid imagery has sucked people of their lives and money from the economy and affected people at large by swallowing schools and hospitals has been well documented in many books such as *The Wolf of Wall Street, Too Big to Fail* and *Money and Power.*

If you think that these monstrous brands can do no harm to you in your daily lives, then think again! Not

[15] J. Freund and E. S. Jacobi, 'Revenge of the Brand Monsters: How Goldman Sachs' Doppelganger Turned Monstrous', *Journal of Marketing Management* 29, no. 1–2 (2013): 175–194.

[16] https://www.investopedia.com/investing/who-is-jordan-belfort/

only do banking scams originate in the most capitalist markets, but these doppelganger brands also have their footprints in the emerging economies. How can we forget the 1992 Bombay Stock Exchange scam engineered by the 'Wolf of the Bombay Stock Exchange', Harshad Shantilal Mehta.[17] Mehta was responsible for the stamp paper scam, bank receipt scam and ready-forward deal scam. Well in the early 1990s, banks were not allowed to invest in stocks; rather, they invested part of their profits in government bonds. But Mehta, acting as a broker to these banks, took their money through his account and invested in stocks and made huge profits. He returned some profits to the bank and kept the rest for himself. Like Jordan Belfort, he also manipulated the stock market with the banks' money to increase stock prices of various companies; for example, ACC stock price shot from ₹200 to ₹9,000 in three months. The public soon realized that Mehta's investments were illegitimate, and his stocks held no value and were just speculated. Many banks were defrauded, and the stock market came crashing down by 72 per cent. The image of banks and stock exchange shattered and the 'big bull' cartoons and media debates created a negative imagery of the stock market and banks which played with the public money for profit. People were not finding it safe to put their money in the banks, as they were not sure if that was a wise investment. To get the banks' credibility back, the government introduced banking reforms and subsequently brought the trust of people back in the banking system of India. Similar cases of Nirav Modi and Vijay Mallya eroded people's trust in the Indian banking system and created a brand doppelganger image of these

---

[17] https://www.indiatoday.in/business/story/harshad-mehta-securities-scam-india-legacy-of-bank-fraud-1733374-2020-10-20

nationalized and private banks.[18] People started circulating hilarious memes and mocked the Indian banking system.

[18] https://economictimes.indiatimes.com/news/india/public-sector-banks-get-hold-of-vijay-mallya-nirav-modi-mehul-choksis-seized-assets-worth-rs-8441-5-crore/articleshow/83771502.cms?from=mdr

Nirav Modi arrested in London

PNB Employees :

Vijay Mallya after hearing Nirav Modi got arrested:

#NiravArrested #NiravModi

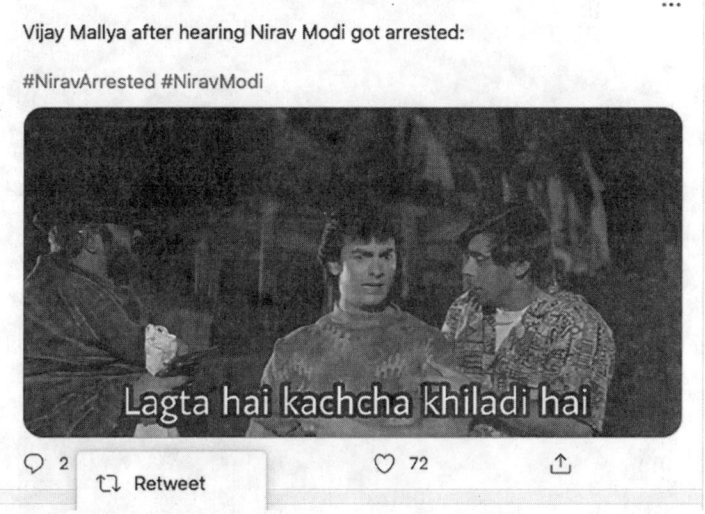

Lagta hai kachcha khiladi hai

💬 2   ⟲ Retweet   ♡ 72   ⬆

In today's dynamic market situation, countering hostile competition, and discerning and ever-demanding customers, the marketers are challenged—the backlash of negative opinions clouds the brand's reputation in the market. This is known as the doppelganger brand image. Before we start formulating strategies to counter these doppelgangers, let's go back to basics in the next chapter and understood how branding truly works!

CHAPTER 2

BRAND NEW WORLD

You now have to decide what 'image' you want for your brand. Image means personality. Products, like people, have personalities, and they can make or break them in the marketplace.

David Ogilvy

When Ray Kroc discovered a small restaurant serving burgers in California in 1954, no one could have believed that the history in branding was going to be written. From a single restaurant to almost 4000 outlets in 119 countries, McDonald's became an iconic brand in over 40 years.[1] Delivering quality, service, cleanliness and value over the last 60 years, it was placed ninth at $129 billion, making it among the 10 most valuable brands in the year 2020. When Mark Zuckerberg, a Harvard student, conceptualized and created a social networking platform for the Harvard students in 2004, little did he know that Facebook will become the biggest

---

[1] https://www.mcdonalds.com/us/en-us/about-us/our-history.html

social networking site with 2.5 billion active users and a brand value with a revenue of around $70.3 billion in the year 2019. When Steve Jobs determined to start Apple in his parent's garage with a couple of friends in 1976, who would have imagined that product innovation coupled with minimalistic designing can make Apple one of the top brands in the world. From Mac to watches, Apple's brand value had grown to $612 billion in 2021 from almost $352 billion in 2020.[2]

When Sunil Bharti Mittal decided to replace the rotary phones with push buttons in 1985, who would have thought that Airtel will become a giant mobile service provider and among the top 10 brands in India with subscribers base of more than 347 million active users.

So what made these brands tick? These are the brands which have always been ahead of their competition. Their products are considered to be better than the rest. They can be ordered from anywhere. Customers are satisfied and loyal to these brands. Such brands have mastered their brand identity and have focused and developed their STAR (BCG matrix) products.

So what do these companies do to create iconic brands?

- Customers want value for their money, and these brands satisfy their needs and wants; in some cases, they delight them at a price they are willing to pay.

- Brands are a set of links in the minds of the customers. These brands, with their clear identity, have over the years cemented their brand associations. So whenever a need arises, the customers think of these brands. So you see 'golden arches' on a highway and you know there is a McDonald's outlet. Similarly, 'Swoosh' reminds of Nike and 'think different' about Apple.

[2] https://www.statista.com/statistics/326052/apple-brand-value/

- Customers' journey from awareness to loyalty is what every brand tends to seek, and these brands are known for their loyal customer base. To earn a loyal customer base, these brands have worked hard to deliver positive brand exposure and experiences. A customer who buys an iPhone will in most cases continue buying an iPad or a Mac or an Apple watch.

- Well, somebody rightly said, 'The companies that get ahead do so because of the way they are run and controlled.' The work environment of these companies encourages innovation and customer centricity aligned with organizational goals. We hear people saying that they would love to work for Google as they say that it is harder to get selected in Google than in Harvard or Oxford.

- They distinguish to gain a competitive advantage. These companies believe in making their competition irrelevant and differentiate the products to provide a superior value to their customers. These brands have a strong unique selling proposition (USP) to position their products. They dramatize their brand ideas and own that idea to differentiate from their competition.

'It takes five times as much to attract a customer than to keep an existing one.'[3] These brands focus on their customers and how they can enhance the lives of their customers. They are consistent with their brand identity and brand communication. Whether on television (TV), radio, newspaper or online, their messages are unanimously conveying one thought, one idea and one reason to buy.

[3] https://hbr.org/2014/10/the-value-of-keeping-the-right-customers

HISTORY OF BRAND

The history of brand dates back to the mid-17th century, and its origin is traced back to the ancient Egypt of 2700 BC, where branding meant to burn and the owners used a hot iron to mark the livestock. It was used to differentiate one group of livestock from another and trace proprietorship in case it gets lost. Since then, brands have been of paramount importance among theorists in the 1980s to develop branding models to understand the building of a brand. The basic theory is to differentiate one product from another and establish ownership. Corporates are no longer building products but building brands. The late 18th century and early 19th century marked the first Industrial Revolution. This saw the transformation of the European and American economies with the focus on mass production with increased efficiency and automatization. Since mass production increased competition and the need to differentiate one product from another, hence came the trademark. The first Trademark Act came in existence in 1881, passed by the US Congress, and branding became an intellectual property, protecting it from competition and copycats. The early 20th century was marked by idea, creativity and technology, when Wright brothers gave wings to their imagination and made the first heavier-than-air 'Wright Flyer' aircraft on 17 December 1903. Since then, many iconic brands have made their way to our mind and heart and continue to do so. Brands like Coca-Cola (1886), Colgate (1873) and Ford Motors (1903) went on air in the early 20th century, with radio being the first electronic medium to air advertisements, and the first radio advertisement went on air on 28 August 1922 on the New York radio station WEAF (now WNBC). The brand was Hawthorne Court apartments in Jackson Heights, selling real estate in Queens, New York.

A 15-minute-long commercial aired at 5.15 PM was scripted as follows[4]:

> Let me enjoin upon you as you value your health and your hopes and your home happiness, get away from the solid masses of brick, where the meager opening admitting a slant of sunlight is mockingly called a light shaft, and where children grow up starved for a run over a patch of grass and the sight of a tree. Thousands of dwellers in the congested district apartments want to remove to healthier and happier sections but they don't know and they can't seem to get into the belief that their living situation and home environment can be improved. Many of them balk at buying a house in the country or the suburbs and becoming a commuter. They have visions of toiling down in a cellar with a sullen furnace, or shoveling snow, or of blistering palms pushing a clanking lawn mower. They can't seem to overcome the pessimistic inertia that keeps pounding into their brains that their crowded, unhealthy, unhappy living conditions cannot be improved.

> The fact is, however, that apartment homes on the tenant-ownership plan can be secured by these city martyrs merely for the deciding to pick them—merely for the devoting of an hour or so to preliminary verification of the living advantages that are within their grasp. And this too within twenty minutes of New York's business center by subway transit.

> Right at your door is such an opportunity. It only requires the will to take advantage of it all. You owe it to yourself and you owe it to your family to leave the hemmed-in, sombre-hued, artificial apartment life of the congested city section and enjoy what nature intended you should enjoy.

---

[4] https://www.britannica.com/topic/WEAF

Dr. Royal S. Copeland, Health Commissioner of New York, recently declared that any person who preached leaving the crowded city for the open country was a public-spirited citizen and a benefactor to the race. Shall we not follow this advice and become the benefactors he praises? Let us resolve to do so. Let me close by urging that you hurry to the apartment home near the green fields and the neighborly atmosphere right on the subway without the expense and the trouble of a commuter, where health and community happiness beckon—the community life and friendly environment that Hawthorne advocated.[5]

Later on, the 1960s–1990s saw the growth of brands and branding.

In India, brands existed even before India's Independence. Jamsetji Tata laid the foundation of Tata Group in 1864 by purchasing a bankrupt oil mill to produce cotton fabric. Dr S. K. Burman, respectfully known as 'Daktar Burman', laid the foundation of one of the leading fast-moving consumer goods (FMCG) companies with a turnover of approx INR 77.5 billion ($1.20 billion). Dr Burman developed ayurvedic medicines to cure the diseases of the villagers around the year 1884. His small clinic has today become one of the world's largest ayurvedic and healthcare companies and has come to be known as Dabur.[6] In the year 1887, an entrepreneur named Ardeshir Godrej decided to quit his law practice and started making locks, and his brother Pirojsha Godrej took the dream forward by diversifying into soaps, etc. Similarly, other great Indian brands such as Rooh Afza (1907) and Parle-G (1929) have contributed significantly to the history of Indian brands.[7]

[5] https://www.getthefourkeys.com/2019/02/20/the-first-radio-commercial/

[6] https://www.dabur.com/amp/in/en-us/about/leadership/our-founder

[7] https://www.financialexpress.com/industry/dabur-india-bets-big-on-direct-distribution/1337925/

PEOPLE DO NOT BUY PRODUCTS, THEY BUY BRANDS

Companies' orientations have moved from the production concept to the marketing concept over the last five decades to understand that consumers will buy those products which are widely available and not so expensive while creating customer value better than competitors'. Business models have evolved over a period. The 1980s witnessed the supply–demand gap, where TVs and refrigerators had to be booked before booking. Distributors and retailers were the king and used to sell the products at huge margins, and that increased their buying powers from companies. Consumers connect with brands emotionally and not by product features. For example, Apple brand equity can make them charge higher price even by providing lesser product features than the competition. They can do away with USB port from laptops or change the ear pod jack and still can come up with a new version at a higher price. Consumers buy brands because of the following reasons:

1. Brands cover consumers' risk.
2. Brands have an emotional connect.
3. Brands save decision-making time.
4. Brands differentiate products.
5. Brands add value to consumers' life.
6. A brand is an expression of a consumer's self.
7. Brands develop communities.

In India, big brands of yesteryears such as BPL, Onida, Videocon and Kelvinator have now become obsolete and reached the decline of their product life cycle many years ago. There were only a few players in the market, and the market was growing. The key players had divided the market share pie and kept their slice intact by attracting and maintaining the most relevant segment for their products. There were clear market leaders, and their dominance could not be challenged. Hindustan Ambassador and Premier Padmini for cars; Onida, Videocon and BPL for white goods; Bajaj, Vespa and LML Piaggio in scooters; and Hero Honda, TVS and Yamaha in motor bikes helped in developing the markets in their respective product categories. The Indian audience was also exposed to TV as a medium of information and entertainment. Doordarshan gave the audience its first pro-social soap opera 'Hum Log' on 7 July 1984. The popularity of this middle-class serial coincided with the growth of the middle-class population in India. The serial plot was weaved around the middle-class struggle and aspirations and drew its inspiration from the Mexican TV serial 'Ven Conmigo'.

BIRTH OF CONSUMERS

Adam Smith stated in his 1776 book *The Wealth of Nations*, 'Consumption is the sole end and purpose of all production.' Although consumers' history can be traced down to the 18th century where people started accumulating gadgets and objects, it got recognition and momentum only after the Second World War. It all started in the United States with the introduction of mail shopping and development of departmental stores owned by the corporates who had the interest of banks on their side to invest capital in the assembly line production of goods which could be used for mass consumption. The sole purpose of retailing the FMCG and durables were to maximize profits. This signified the democratization of individual desires and consumption by choice. Historian Frederick Allen synthesized the Marxist and Keynes theories in his book *Can Capitalist Last?* and made a point that the deficient aggregate demand is a contradiction to capitalism.

He wrote, 'Business had learned as never before the importance of the ultimate consumer. Unless he could be persuaded to buy and buy lavishly, the whole stream of six-cylinder cars, super heterodynes, cigarettes, rouge compacts and electric ice boxes would be dammed up at its outlets.' Increase in electrification of houses in the United States from 35 per cent to 68 per cent between 1921 and 1929 raised the demand for electrical gadgets such as vacuum cleaners, radios and refrigerators. The same period saw the demand for cars going up by around 350 per cent. Even in Britain and Australia, similar trends were observed but with a small base of population. Consumerism 1.0 was short-lived due to risk borrowing and reckless lending which saw the collapse of the first wave of consumerism. And then came the Great Depression in 1930, followed by the Second World War between 1939 and 1945, bringing the growth of consumerism to a halt or going into negative. In 1955, economist and retail analyst Victor Lebow remarked,

> Our enormously productive economy demands that we make consumption our way of life, that we convert the buying and use of goods into rituals, that we seek our spiritual satisfaction, our ego satisfaction, in consumption…. We need things consumed, burned up, replaced and discarded at an ever-accelerating rate.[8]

Efforts through advertising and sales promotion to create demand and increase consumerism were made by corporates, accelerating the growth of Consumerism 2.0. The increase in consumerism led to the increase in brands or vice versa, and brands gave consumers not only the reason to buy but also incentives to buy to increase consumption.

....

[8] https://davidsuzuki.org/story/consumer-society-no-longer-serves-needs/#:~:text=Retailing%20analyst%20Victor%20Lebow%20famously,our%20ego%20satisfaction%20in%20consumption.

INDIAN MIDDLE CLASS: A HUGE MARKET

The history of the Indian middle class can be traced 200 years back[9] during the British Raj in the 18th century. During that period, the middle class emerged due to change in the socio-economic policies and rise of new professions. The new professions got introduced due to the Industrial Revolution and modernization of the work process, bringing in Western influence on the capitalistic and commercial progress. The socio-economic and political systems were against the growth of capitalism, and hence people believed in stocking wealth rather than investing in trade or other economic activities. So the middle class during the British regime comprised of clerks, supervisors, contractors, brokers, moneylenders, industrial workers and the educated middle class of professionals. Besides the British who invested to develop the Indian industry, there were few Bengalis in Kolkata and Parsis in Mumbai who were responsible for shaping up the future of industries in India. Since then, the Indian middle class is responsible for the growth of the Indian consumer market.

The middle class today comprises half of the Indian population. Unlike the shrinking middle-class population in Europe and North America, the Indian middle class is increasing, leading to a rise in consumption. This has attracted many brands to invest in India to capitalize on the growing consumer market, which is estimated to be at $4 trillion by 2025. The consumption patterns are riding on the low Internet rates (thanks to Jio entry) and speed of networks, making the Indian middle class spend on lifestyle products. Companies such as Amazon, Walmart and Netflix have ploughed

[9] B. B. Misra, *The Indian Middle Classes: Their Growth in Modern Times* (Bombay: Oxford University Press, 1963).

billions of dollars to woe the Indian middle class. With Walmart buying 77 per cent stakes in Flipkart and Amazon eyeing on the food business of Aditya Birla Group, the battle of royal brands is just around the corner. Researchers have found out that it is the consumers' habits that drive consumption in any economy. Consumers are generally loyal to their shopping patterns, as they will for their daily needs call or visit the nearest grocery store or enjoy home delivery of their favourite restaurant meal. Brand advertising supports the predictability of their shopping behaviour, and occasional sales promotion gives them the incentive to buy. E-commerce companies are redefining consumer behaviour and breaking the consumer habit forms. The middle class of the emerging economies is finding itself with more disposable income and digitally convenient ways to purchase. Philip Kotler's 4 P model (product, price, place and promotion) has to adapt to the changing consumer buying patterns. Brands need to realign their marketing strategies to these new-age consumers who influence product development, decide on the channel to buy, use their buyers' power to reduce price and force companies to adjust their promotional mix.

CUSTOMER TOUCHPOINTS

Today, customers are empowered, and touchpoint marketing is the way forward for brand engagements. For example, a bank manages to influence customers' emotions at each touchpoint—phone banking, website, sales desk, account opening, banking hall, customer service desk, tellers, branch manager, ATM, net banking, mobile banking, relationship managers, etc. Therefore, it is critical to understand your customers' touchpoints offline and online to build a long-lasting relationship.

BRAND TOUCHPOINTS

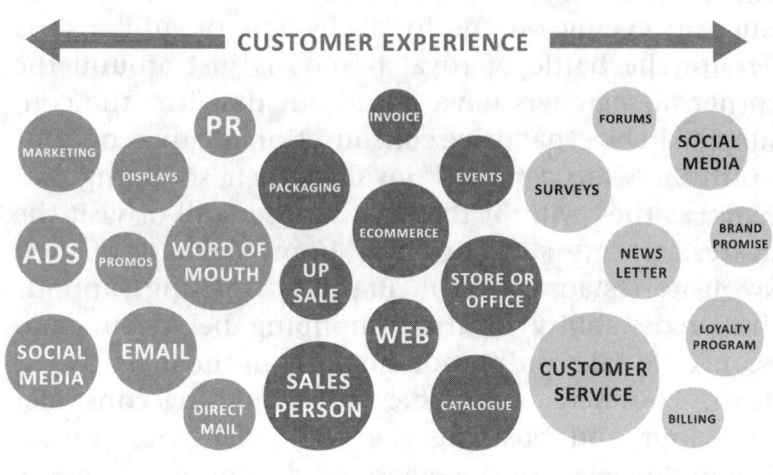

Source: wotsthebigidea.com[10]

Consumers have formulated new ways to connect with the brands of their choice. They are going beyond the control of the manufacturers or retailers. This is leading to new engagement strategies by the marketers to develop and maintain long-term relationships with their customers. The consumer decision journey has evolved mainly due to the digitalization of the economy. Therefore, consumer touchpoints have become more important than the large number of budgets allocated to the media mix.

ADVERTISING BUILDS BRANDS

> *When I write an advertisement, I don't want you to tell me that you find it 'creative'. I want you to find it so interesting that you buy the product.*
>
> David Ogilvy

Troll Proof Branding in the Age of Doppelgangers

[10] https://www.bcg.com/publications/2019/dividends-digital-marketing-maturity

From advertisements promoting Buddha's teaching by Ashoka the Great around 263 BCE, advertising has come a long way. Rocks and pillar edicts were used as a form of advertising by the great emperor to spread Buddhism. *Bengal Gazette* was the first print newspaper (1780) from Calcutta, and soon the government advertisements saw the light in the earlier newspapers published from Calcutta. The 19th century saw the emergence of the pioneer advertising agencies such as Hindustan Thompson Associates (HTA; 1929) and Lintas (1939). Both the agencies brought a significant amount of strategic and creative insights into advertising, which we see today. Indian advertising has evolved for the last eight decades and has given us some of the most iconic advertising campaigns. We have come a long way since the HTA Lux toilet soap's first advertisement featuring Leela Chitnis in 1941, followed by many Bollywood celebrities including two male actors Shah Rukh Khan and Abhishek Bachchan endorsing the soap as a secret of their beauty. Another iconic character created by HTA in 1946 was Air India's Maharaja mascot.[11] Bobby Kooka, the then commercial director of the airline, and Umesh Rao, an artist with HTA, created the iconic symbol, which till date is the identity of the airline.

These campaigns have not only built brands but also made the people behind them ad gurus. Among India's top ad gurus standing tall is Piyush Pandey (Ogilvy & Mather [O&M]) known for popular ads such as Cadbury's 'Kuch Khaas Hai' and Fevicol's 'Fevicol Ka Mazboot Jod' and recently for slogans such as 'Ab Ki Baar, Modi Sarkaar', 'Bahut Hua Bhrashtachaar, Ab Ki Baar, Modi Sarkaar' and 'Bahut Hui Mahengayi Ki Vaar, Ab ki Baar, Modi Sarkaar'.

---

[11] https://www.thebetterindia.com/127991/air-india-maharajah-mascot-bobby-kooka-story/

On Bharatiya Janata Party's (BJP) win in the 2014 elections and as the man behind the BJP's advertising campaign, Piyush Pandey credited the BJP's success to the 'fantastic product' that it had as Narendra Modi and his ability to communicate with people.

'The clincher of any campaign is the product. No campaign can sell a bad product,' said Piyush Pandey.

The man behind the Coca-Cola campaign 'Thanda Matlab Coca-Cola', a rural catchphrase for cold drinks (which won an award at Cannes) is a poet, lyricist, scriptwriter and adman—Prasoon Joshi. An IMT Ghaziabad MBA graduate and creative director of McCann, Prasoon Joshi rose to great heights from the 'king of jingles' to Bollywood movies' celebrity dialogue writer and songwriter (*Rang De Basanti* and *Tare Zameen Par*).

EMOTIONS SELL

Advertising in India has been the most important promotional mix to build brands. Ad gurus such as Alyque Padamsee, Piyush Pandey and Prahlad Kakkar and brand strategists such as Santosh Desai, Anisha Motwani and Hari Krishnan have been working hard and intelligently and tapping into consumers' emotions to sell their brands. Researches have proved that most of our purchase decisions are irrational and emotional as compared to logical decision-making. Unlike robots who work on mechanical logical reasoning, we human beings, by design, are more irrational in our purchase decision-making. As humans, we are not true to our buying behaviour, as we are more often governed by our subconscious urges known as emotions. Emotions are what drives our purchase decision, and brand managers and advertising professionals exploit this by launching emotional campaigns. In the year 1980, renowned psychologist Robert Plutchik created the 'wheel of emotions' and illustrated how emotions are related to each other.

This set of emotions has been the core of brand campaigns and has been a successful formula in connecting consumers with the brand. For example, luxury brands try to influence our emotions associated with self-worth and social status. Mobile phones tickle our emotions of connecting with friends and family. Sports brands such as Nike and Adidas inspire confidence and a sense of achievement by being competitive. Many other brands like Havells use an emotional platform to launch their proposition 'Wires That Don't Catch Fire'.[12] Dwelling on the mother–son relationship and how a son can't see his mother in pain, the advertisement misuses this emotion and builds a storyline around it. In the TVC, a mother is burning her finger every time she flips a roti (Indian bread) on fire. The son could not see her in pain and gets a Havells wire and bends it to make a tong to flip the roti. Targeted at electricians, the ad was able to generate an emotional response and communicate its proposition effectively.

Emotions sell! Brands are no more a symbol, name, logo or tagline but have gone beyond the physiological attributes to psychological attributes. Marketers have figured out by now that consumers do not buy products, they buy brands.

THE BATTLE OF BRANDS GOES DIGITAL

The battle of brands has shifted now to the Internet. The digital economy has raised the expectations of consumers, and brands need to adjust their branding strategies

---

[12] https://www.adgully.com/havells-releases-new-tvc-for-wires-that-don-t-catch-fire-79734.html

to respond to these growing new-age consumers. Digitalization is changing how consumers choose to buy. Companies are now ripening in their digital marketing path. Brand marketing is becoming more data-driven than ever. The data is captured at each stage of customer touchpoint and digital footprints.

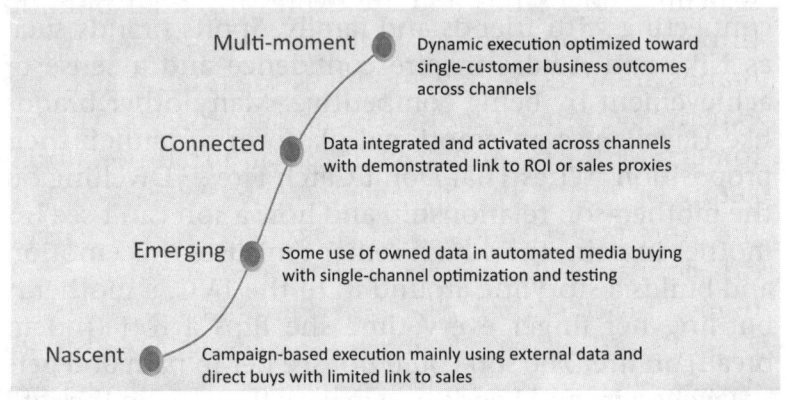

Source: Boston Consulting Group.[13]

Boston Consulting Group (BCG) believes that companies which walk the path of digital marketing maturity transformation could witness a 20 per cent rise in revenues and 30 per cent savings in cost efficiency.[14] This transformation is more relevant, as India is reaching more than 450 million Internet users and is the second-largest online market, next to China. By 2021, 59 per cent of India will be online through almost 2 billion devices.[15] The consumers' screen time is increasing and screen sizes are reducing from a 32-inch

[13] https://www.bcg.com/publications/2019/dividends-digital-marketing-maturity

[14] https://www.bcg.com/publications/2019/dividends-digital-marketing-maturity

[15] https://wearesocial.com/blog/2020/01/digital-2020-3-8-billion-people-use-social-media

TV to a 6-inch smartphone. Brands are seeing this as an opportunity to create engagement with consumers by creating platforms for UGC and developing online communities.

Customers are freewheeling their choices and are engaging with brands in a completely new way. They are searching for brands and are expressing their opinions through various online platforms like never before. Brands are working day and night to enhance customer experience through multi-screen engagements. The customers' journey is no more linear, and traditional marketing strategies are no longer effective to connect with the more evolved individual customer. An earlier brand can connect with customers within a stipulated time frame, but now they need to communicate with them 24 × 7 × 365 days. Gone are the days when in 1980's doordarshan, India's only National TV channel was the only medium for the brands to reach out to their consumers. A lot of money was spilled over in advertising and reached out to consumers who were not the target audience with the sheer nature of the medium and the choices of channels. Today, consumers expect more personalized communication and more evolved engagements with the brand. The media options were limited with few nationalized newspapers like *The Times of India* and more of vernaculars or regional print media such as *The Hindu, Hindustan Times, The Telegraph, Ajit* and *Punjab Kesari*. Radio options were limited to All India Radio and TV to Doordarshan and later moved to cable TV. TV was considered to provide the audiovisual brand experience and make an emotional connection with the consumers, whereas print media was to be used to give details about the product and list of dealers from where a customer could buy the brand, and radio was used as a trigger and reminder of the integrated marketing campaign.

Customers today do not buy once; they keep on coming back in terms of product replacement, upgrades and services. Therefore, marketers are orchestrating customer engagement campaigns at each of the consumer touchpoints. Marketers have now realized that the traditional marketing funnel no longer works and is replaced by the customers' life cycle. The customer decision journey has evolved; they have far more options, information and multi-channel engagements to make a buying choice. Media consumption has seen an upsurge mainly due to smartphone penetration.

Customers want information and entertainment on the go with smartphones, whose sale had globally reached 1.5 billion by 2020.[16] The traditional marketing model has become outdated, and a new version of the consumer decision journey has replaced this in the form of the digital age. Consumers now consider brands based on their exposure to various touchpoints and their perceptions and evaluation of brands; they arrive at a brand list and select the brand of their choice at the point of purchase. The brand engagement does not stop here, and there is a continuous dialogue between the customer and the brand, leading to a rich brand experience. This further based on a positive brand experience leads to repeated buying or the loyalty loop, resulting in recurrence of revenue from the same customer.

Customers' expectations from their brands are increasing, and they are constantly in talks with their chosen brand all time through their smartphones. They lean on brand reviews to help them in making a sound brand buying decision.

[16] https://www.statista.com/statistics/263437/global-smartphone-sales-to-end-users-since-2007/

Loyalty Loop

Source: McKinsey & Company.[17]

'If you make customers unhappy in the physical world, they might each tell six friends. If you make customers unhappy on the Internet, they can each tell 6,000,' says Jeff Bezos.

THE EMPOWERED CONSUMER

Not only creative strategies but also media consumption habits have a great influence on branding strategies. Media planning agencies no longer characterize the population based on its demographic characteristics but are looking more at their behavioural patterns of viewership or readership than their age. For most marketers now, age is just a number. As technology becomes more and more accessible, marketers are not only closing down on the 18–35 age bracket but are also going deeper into their consumption behavioural patterns. Netflix, for example, has 75,00 different content genres based on its viewers' consumption patterns. The way consumers absorb news and entertainment has transformed the way content is

[17] https://www.mckinsey.com/business-functions/marketing-and-sales/our-insights/the-consumer-decision-journey

delivered. Consumers are streaming more content on their computers or mobile phones than watching it on TV. The Internet has revamped media consumption patterns. Traditionally, news and entertainment were a household phenomenon through cable or newspaper. Families used to get together to watch 'Mahabharata' or 'Ramayana', and one newspaper was split into news and sports pages. But with the growth of smartphones, entertainment has become an individual affair. Marketing to one and then spreading it to many is the strategic goal of the current marketing honchos. The digital consumption of the content has led to the creation of big data of consumption patterns, compelling the marketers to apply complex algorithms to engage and retain digital customers. New data science models are used to customize the content according to the taste and preference of the discerning digital customers.

Consumers are empowered, and the way they use the Internet, mobile phones, social media and e-commerce gives us completely new insights into their digital consumer behaviour. The year 2021 added 80 million digital users, making 59.5 per cent of the population digital.[18] An average Internet user spends almost 145 minutes a day, with most of this time spent on various social media networks. E-commerce is giving way to m-commerce, as more and more people are using mobile phones to shop and mobile wallets to transact online.

Brand communication is no longer a one-way street; consumers interact with brands and can even help marketers in their brand-building efforts or otherwise. Purchase decisions and brand preferences are not only influenced by the brand's communication but more and

---

[18] https://datareportal.com/reports/digital-2021-global-overview-report

more people are influenced by peer reviews. That is why the role of UGC is gaining preference over company-generated brand communication. Research have found out that 66 per cent of people refer to normal people's brand experience stories rather than celebrity-endorsed brand stories. So an Amitabh Bachchan-featured advertisement will have less credibility over social media reviews by existing consumers. Therefore, top brands are increasing their spending on UGC campaigns by asking customers to generate ideas and viral them through their social network. So if you are planning to travel and book a hotel, you would prefer to see the photos posted by customers than the hotel itself.

The 'share a coke' campaign just did that by printing 150 most common names on the Coca-Cola bottle and asked customers to share it with their near and dear ones.[19] Customers went gaga over the idea and started sharing a photograph with the coke bottle on their social media network, making the campaign an instant hit. Similarly, Apple launched its #shotonIphone campaign keeping in mind the customer pain point of not being able to capture a clear picture in low lights through an iPhone. To regain customer confidence, Apple started this campaign to make people take pictures in low light and post it online. Apple ran the campaign almost three long years through UGC and was able to regain the faith of its customers.

UGC is not always positively inclined towards promoting the brand. A customer may have a good perception or experience with the brand and vice versa. Many times, customers have been able to damage the reputation of a brand through a negative UGC. There are many

---

[19] https://www.coca-colacompany.com/au/faqs/what-was-the-share-a-coke-campaign

examples to prove the point that people try to jam the brand messages by using memes, etc., and creating a negative image of a brand. In the following chapters, we will understand how brand doppelganger imagery is created through various means and how to tackle it so that brands today can be the best versions of themselves.

CHAPTER 3

BRAND STRATEGIES GONE WRONG

Branding demands commitment;
commitment to continual re-invention;
striking chords with people to stir their
emotions; and commitment to imagination.
It is easy to be cynical about such things,
much harder to be successful.

Sir Richard Branson, founder of
Virgin Group, business magnate,
author, investor and philanthropist

Branding is a key component of any business strategy. Although people sometimes confuse branding with advertising, advertising is just a tool to build brands. Branding is a strategy to create customer value by gaining a competitive advantage. It is a cultural story about the brand circulated in the society. When circulated among the popular culture, a product acquires meaning in the eyes of the consumer, and this meaning is known as brand. Brand managers try to quantitatively assign a value to this meaning, but for consumers, it is more perceptual. So when brand elements are circulated in popular culture, they gain meaning through consumer experiences. Then brands are not only recognized but also recalled by their brand elements such as logo and name and build deeper cultural associations. McDonald's name, Nike's Swoosh logo and Titan's signature violin tune are not merely pieces of brand elements but are also key components of the brand culture. They inspire their users. Facebook, Flipkart, Tata, Apple and Samsung are examples of successful brands which have created strong value in the eyes of their stakeholders. But why do some brands succeed and some don't? According to Booz Allen Hamilton, most companies believe that their brand is the key component of their success and hence they constantly need to keep on developing branding strategies to gain a competitive advantage.

Over the years, companies have been practising various branding strategies to build a strong brand. Although there is no set formula for building brands, some guiding principles have emerged from the success stories of strong brands. Sometimes people misunderstand branding strategies for marketing strategies. Although both kinds of strategies are connected, their spectrum is different. as marketing strategies generally involve four key factors—4 Ps (product, price, place and promotion)—known as the 'marketing mix'.

Marketing mix is defined as a 'set of marketing tools that the firm uses to pursue its marketing objectives in the target market',[1] whereas branding is to create a strong perception about the product in the minds of the customers. Let's look at some good marketing strategies before we understand the branding strategies and how they have evolved over time. One of the examples of a

---

[1] P. Kotler, *Marketing Management* (Millennium Edition), Custom Edition for University of Phoenix (Hoboken, NJ: Prentice Hall, 2000), 9.

good product strategy, the first 'P' of marketing mix, is of a toothpaste company—how a simple product innovation without any cost can increase sales by 40–50 per cent. This company in the 1950s was looking for ideas to increase its market share and grow the category of its toothpaste brand.[2] Therefore, they were looking for ideas through a competition involving prize money. One contestant came and told them that he had the idea which could increase the toothpaste brand sale by 40 per cent without any additional marketing cost. The management was sceptical about this idea not involving any marketing cost, so they shunned this man's proposal. Time went by and nothing seemed to strike the management, so at last, they called this man and asked him about his idea to increase sales. The man gave them an envelope containing a small piece of paper and on that only four words were written: 'make the hole bigger'. It meant that just by increasing the diameter of the nozzle from 5 mm to 6 mm, the consumer would use more toothpaste with every squeeze. History was created!

Researchers further attempted to draw a correlation between product durability and market share. In 2014, two Chinese researchers Lemin Wu and Yuheng Zhao did an empirical analysis of this phenomenon and concluded that companies in monopolistic competition usually overextend the product durability such as cars. So basically they were saying that because consumers have shifting loyalties, the companies should try to extend the durability of the product so that they could sell more services. But since toothpaste is considered to be a durable product, in monopolistic competition, companies are not sure if the customer would repurchase their product. So brands like Honda know that the

---

[2] Ibid.

customer may or may not buy their car again. Hence, the tendency is to make the car more durable so that they can earn from servicing it over the lifetime of the product. But the research proved that this may not be true for products like toothpaste, particularly when the company has a large market share in the product category. Therefore, the empirical research proved that there is a negative correlation between durability and market share, particularly for the companies with large market share. This is very clear from the fact that any company with a huge market share would like customers to buy more and more of their products and hence would reduce the durability of the product.

Not only products but brands have also used pricing as a tool to gain a competitive advantage. Generally, there are five types of pricing strategies—cost-plus pricing, value-based pricing, competitive pricing, skimming and penetration pricing strategies. These can be understood by picking up any marketing textbook. But we need to understand one thing, that is, economics and psychology play a great role in any marketing strategy and in this case it is both. The above five strategies come straight from economic models, but there is psychological pricing which is based on the assumption that customers buy emotionally and not all buying decisions are rational. One such example is when brands are priced at $0.99 or $0.85, rather than $1. This is because when an item is priced at $0.99 instead of $1.00, customers react to the first number, which in this case is 0 and 1, and think that the first option is cheaper than the second, even though there is very little cost difference. Over the years, retailers have been influencing (read manipulating) our spending habits by various pricing tactics, for example, BOGO (buy one get one) free and anchoring (their price ₹450, our price ₹245). Apple uses the 'decoy pricing' strategy with great effect to influence customer preference towards one product by introducing another product as a decoy. Apple launched iPhone X first time with a four-digit price in the United States. The question was: Would people shell out $1,000 just for a phone? So Apple introduced iPhone 8 as a decoy, which was a slight upgrade from iPhone 7 in terms of battery life and updated camera but no thrills from a customer's point of view. Therefore, their preference moved towards iPhone X, and iPhone 8 only acted as a decoy to influence customer preference. This becomes clear when we compare the price differences and launch date. iPhone 7 was launched on 16 September 2016, iPhone 8 on 29 September 2017 and iPhone X on 3 November 2017. So the idea of launching iPhone 8 was simply to prepare customers to buy a high-priced iPhone X. Then there is 'centre stage pricing'. According to this pricing strategy, consumers tend to choose the product which is displayed in the centre in line with other products. Therefore, companies place their most expensive product in the middle to increase its probability to be preferred. Many e-commerce sites use the 'framing effect' pricing strategy, where through comparison with other products they show how much a customer will save.

The channel of distribution strategies is used by many marketers to push a product on the customer to buy. Most learnt professionals know basic distribution strategies such as direct, indirect, intensive, exclusive and selected distribution through retailers or distributors or directly to customers. Many companies aim to reduce customers' costs and risk through downstream activities in order to gain competitive advantage. For instance, a can of Pepsi may cost you ₹30–₹40 at a modern trade outlet such as Spencer and Reliance Mart, whereas you may end up paying ₹100 for the same in a mall or a movie hall. Therefore, to satisfy customers' extraordinary demands, companies want to ensure that they get what they want by experimenting with their distribution channels by making them more flexible and responsive. Take for example Walmart, the largest retailer with a net worth of $520 billion in the year 2020.[3] With 783 million sq. ft of retail and 143 sq. ft of distribution centres, Walmart has achieved leadership stature for its 'best-in-class' distribution and supply chain operations. Each distribution centre serves around 100 retail stores spread over an area of 250 mi. Walmart's fast and responsive truck fleet takes maximum two days to supply goods to retail stores and replenish store shelves twice a week. The success of Walmart can be attributed to its transportation system which is the backbone of its distribution strategy. The logistics system practised by Walmart is known as cross-docking, in which goods are picked up from the suppliers' manufacturing base, sorted, and distributed straight to the customers. Mainly five cross-docking systems are followed by Walmart:

1. **Opportunistic cross-docking:** Mapping the requirement of each store cross-docking requires Walmart to procure the exact quantity required by the store and ship it just in time to avoid any storage cost.

2. **Flow-through cross-docking:** For a product that is perishable and has a short shelf life, Walmart's transportation makes sure that there is a constant inflow and outflow of goods and services which are difficult to store in the distribution centres.

3. **Distributor cross-docking:** In this system, the manufacturer directly supplies the goods to the retailer involving no intermediaries.

[3] https://www.statista.com/statistics/183399/walmarts-net-sales-world wide-since-2006/

4. **Manufacturer cross-docking:** In this docking system, the manufacturer acts as a mini warehouse or a mini distribution centre.

5. **Pre-allocated cross-docking:** In this system, the manufacturer produces the products, packs and labels it, and delivers it to Walmart's distribution centres.

The reason behind Walmart's competitive prices is their use of buying power to negotiate with suppliers based on large quantities of orders and their flexible distribution and supply chain channel. Walmart buys in such large quantities that their dedicated truck fleet cost of distribution is marginal and helps in keeping the prices low to gain a competitive advantage.

The second-largest US retailer giving tough competition to the leader Walmart is Amazon, which has recorded $386 billion of annual revenue, and with pandemic, it has upped its revenue by a whopping 38 per cent around $100 billion compared to 2020.[4] The company's strengths are its innovative technologies and high proficiency in distribution and supply chain management. Continuing with constant technological innovation, Amazon has many firsts to its name, as Jeff Bezos summarized in his comment,

> Amazon is what it is because of the invention. We do crazy things together and then make them normal. We pioneered customer reviews, 1-Click, personalized recommendations, Prime's insanely-fast shipping, Just Walk Out shopping, the Climate Pledge, Kindle, Alexa, Marketplace, infrastructure cloud computing, Career Choice, and much more.[5]

---

[4] https://www.forbes.com/sites/shelleykohan/2021/02/02/amazons-net-profit-soars-84-with-sales-hitting-386-billion/

[5] https://finance.yahoo.com/news/amazons-secret-success-doing-crazy-215217907.html

From a small online bookseller, the company has grown remarkably due to its highly efficient supply chain. Redefining supply chain management, Amazon has outpassed its competition and has been a game changer in the online retail industry. Most importantly, it has a controlled supply chain and has mastered the last-mile delivery to the customers' doorstep, leading to a high level of customer satisfaction. It has been raising the benchmark by shortening the shipping time from a two-day delivery to a one-hour shipment through 'Amazon Prime Now' service. This is possible because Amazon does not depend on third-party logistics and has insourcing logistics to make such a quick delivery through its in-house resources. The innovative strategies surprise Amazon's competition, as when they try to catch up with one strategy, it raises the bar with yet another innovative strategy and stays ahead of the competition all along. Further, Amazon outsources its inventory management to the third party particularly for those items which are not so frequently ordered. The share of the revenue pie for these items is around 50 per cent of its revenue. Also, besides giving customers cash-on-delivery payment options, Amazon empowers its customers with some time or money-saving delivery options such as Prime delivery, one-day delivery, first-class delivery and free super-saver delivery. To reduce its dependency on third-party vendors such as FedEx and UPS for delivery, Amazon has started a new programme called 'Delivery Service Partner' to equip people to manage their delivery using Amazon's technological and logistics support. So what Amazon does is forecast the region-wise demand and bring its warehouses closer to metro cities. The warehouses are fully automatic through a robotic warehouse solution known as Kiva Systems. Keeping the future strategy of expanding its supply chain and building its own transportation network in mind, it is expanding its Boeing 767 fleet. Eyeing big, Amazon's CEO Jeff Bezos is planning a drone-based delivery system known as Amazon Prime Air. Like Domino's', to ensure delivery of Amazon packets to a radius of 10 mi within 30 minutes, Amazon will deliver packets less than 5 pounds (around 2 kg).

Promotion plays a very important role in building brands. An effective promotional strategy involving a promotional mix such as advertising, sales promotion, direct marketing, public relation (PR) and digital marketing will make your brand communication message reach out to your target audience and will influence their purchase preference and eventually persuade them to buy your product or services. Every component of the promotional mix has its value and can be strategically used to promote a company or its offerings. Since the last one decade or two, companies are integrating these promotional tools to maximize effectiveness and drive efficiency in brand promotional campaigns. Integrated marketing communication (IMC) requires seamless coordination and integration of all or a few communication tools (print, electronic and digital) to engage consumers at each touchpoint to drive maximum effectiveness. Red Bull integrated their PR campaign with YouTube for their most brave and adventurous PR campaign—Red Bull Stratos. By sponsoring Felix Baumgartner's record-breaking freefall from 128,000 ft above the ground and him becoming the first human to break the sound barrier in freefall, Red Bull registered an incredible PR extreme stunt. It live-streamed the jump on YouTube and not on TV as they targeted the youth and lived to its brand positioning that 'Red Bull Gives You Wings'. This was an amazing integration of traditional communication tools like PR with the digital medium YouTube. This gave the brand huge print and electronic media coverage all over the world and increased its followers on social media by many folds. The brand became the most trending topic on social media for weeks and 8 million people watched the YouTube live-streaming. They also built a social sharing website, updating each frame of the jump as it happened.

Another of my favourite IMC campaigns is the iconic 'Got Milk?' campaign by California Milk Processor Board and the San Francisco-based advertising agency Goodby, Silverstein & Partners (GS&P). Well, it all started when the milk consumption in the state of California dropped to 6 per cent between 1987 and 1992. The consumption habits were shifting towards juices, iced tea, cola drinks and coffee, and this led to lower consumption of milk. Also, milk was considered to be more of a beverage for children, and as children reached their teenage, they wanted to have more drinks consumed by adults such as coffee and colas. Milk promotion was left to the National Dairy Board and California Milk Processor Board, who ended up spending merely $13 million to encourage consumption of dairy products. This was too less when compared with Coca-Cola, which was spending more than $100 million annually on their Coca-Cola Classic brand. Despite creating a campaign 'Milk ... It Does a Body Good', targeting the non-milk drinker through its advertising agency McCann Erickson in the 1980s, milk consumption still dropped from 30 to 24.1 gallons per person annually. So the new agency on record GS&P after their focus group test on the milk drinkers concluded that the consumers wanted milk only when they ran out of it. In other words, deprivation of milk was the cause of knowing the value of it when consumers started missing it. It's like if you are having sandwiches or cookies or cereals and you discover that you don't have milk in your refrigerator is when you want it. So a campaign 'Got Milk?' was developed around this finding, and $23 million during that time was budgeted for the

IMC campaign. The campaign starred Hollywood actors, politicians and sportspersons and within one year the sale of milk jumped by 7 per cent. One of the advertisements showed a celebrity eating a sandwich and also listening to a radio talk show running out of milk. The radio jockey threw a quiz question, 'Who shot Alexander Hamilton?' The man looked at the portrait on his wall that showed Burr and the bullet he had used to kill Hamilton. Because he ran out of milk, the man garbled, 'Aaawwon Buuuhh', with a mouth full of sandwich (which he couldn't swallow without milk) and then the tagline 'Got Milk?' The 1990s witnessed the celebrity culture, and the 'Got Milk?' campaign made the best use of this pop culture. When milk was considered to be boring, only for children and to have more fat, this iconic campaign came out with the 'Milk Mustache' campaign. Riding on the celebrity culture and addressing the brand problem of people losing interest in milk as a product, this campaign involved all the celebrity influencers from all spheres to wear a milk moustache and promote the drinking of milk. From Bill Clinton to Naomi Campbell to Britney Spears, the milk moustache was worn by all to promote the cause. Over 20 years, around 350 celebrities including Dilbert cartoon characters endorsed the milk moustache to promote the drinking of milk.

Well, there are numerous examples of great advertising and promotions which have even made it to the Cannes gold category from all over the world.

Today, we consume so many of these iconic brands in our day-to-day life. We are influenced by their marketing genius and eventually buy these products. We prefer to buy branded products, as it reduces our risk of buying a quality product which will perform as per our expectation or as promised by the brand makers. We always try to buy a known brand over an unknown brand to reduce functional, social–psychological and, ultimately, financial risks. So branding is a very important element of a company's marketing strategy. Marketers always have two contradictory objectives in mind: differentiate their brands from the competition and make them central to the product category they belong to. Brands such as Maggi in instant noodles, Cadbury Dairy Milk in chocolates, Coca-Cola in soft drinks and McDonald's in fast food are the ones which are at the top of mind in the category. These brands are responsible for defining the dynamics of the product category, shaping consumer preferences, setting industry pricing and developing the category. To build an iconic brand, a brand has to have a strategy. A branding strategy usually is to differentiate the brand from the competition and gain a competitive advantage by increasing brand equity. Although there are financial and consumer-based brand equity models to measure the brand equity, it all boils down to how strong, unique and favourable the brand associations are in the minds of the consumers. So let's look at some of the few branding strategies which the companies have adopted to influence the perception of their consumers and compelled them to buy their brands.

CREATING A BETTER MOUSETRAP

> Build a better mousetrap and the world
> will beat a path to your door.
>
> Ralph Waldo Emerson

Here, Emerson meant that if you create a great product, everyone is going to buy it. Therefore, to 'build a better mousetrap' is to create a product or servicing offer which the customer cannot refuse and will reach out to buy.

It also refers to the fact that you keep on innovating and improving your current product or services by increasing its efficiency and performance. This has been the approach right from the time of the Industrial Revolution in the 1700s originating from Britain, where mass products were made by using new energy and techniques to build products which were superior to its previous versions of the technology. Germany, for long, believed in such kind of marketing. Its motto has been that 'We will give you the best of the product through our cutting-edge engineering whether its cars, white goods are heavy engineering products.' Philip Kotler, the great marketing guru, calls it a 'product-centric approach'. Back in the time, Henry Ford completely discarded customer opinion in product development by quoting, 'If I'd have asked my customers what they wanted, they would have told me "A faster horse"'. Keeping this philosophy of his, Ford motors developed an assembly line for mass production which reduced the time taken to build a car from 12 hours to 1 hour and 33 minutes. This philosophy of Henry Ford was an inspiration to Steve Jobs, who quoted, 'You can't just ask customers what they want and then try to give that to them. By the time you get it built, they'll want something new.' Thomas Edison, Henry Ford and Steve Jobs were all outliers and believed that with research and development, you can produce a great product and people will seek it. Influenced by Americans and The Toyota Way, Japanese adopted kaizen, which means 'continuous improvement'. Masaaki Imai in his book *Kaizen: The Key to Japan's Competitive Success* explains kaizen's 16 principles with 15 case studies to demonstrate how Japanese businesses have adopted continuous product and process improvements to gain a competitive advantage. The biggest learning from the Japanese firms is that they challenged their own best practices and continuously improved on them as they believed that any best practice is created in a certain social, economic, technological and political environment and since these keep on constantly changing, the best practices need to be revisited and must be improved on creating new best business practices. The best example of kaizen is Toyota, where an engineering graduate only moves to the next level if he masters the art of picking up the same pair of nuts and bolts from a box. To focus on increasing efficiency, Toyota focuses on 'muscle memory', so that the engineers' hands work with unfailing precision.

Similarly, German engineering is world-renowned. They believe in high precision-engineered products in automobile, medical, chemical, mechanical and electrical engineering. Did you know that Albert Einstein was a German-born theoretical physicist, Rudolf Diesel, famous for inventing the diesel engine, was a German mechanical engineer, and MP3 and electron microscope are Germany's invention? With its cutting-edge engineering, Germany created the mousetrap which saw the emergence of the world's leading companies such as DaimlerChrysler, Volkswagen, Bosch, Mercedes, KHD Humboldt, Audi and BMW earning huge profits.

But all this product-centric approach still has an element of 'knowing your customers'. Whether it's Steve Jobs or Henry Ford, they all created products beyond the need realized by their customers. They focused on the functional benefits as a differentiator. Functional benefits are based on product attributes that satisfied the functional utility need of the customers. Dove soap is a good example of using moisturizer as its functional differentiator to create a mousetrap for its customers. Dove came into existence after the Second World War in the United States and was initially not marketed as a soap, as its formula came from the military where Dove was used as a skin cleanser for burns and wounds with a high level of moisturizer in it. The year 1957 saw Dove's first campaign developed by O&M, claiming it to be a soap with one-quarter cleansing cream for dry skin treatment.

BUT IS DEVELOPING A BETTER MOUSETRAP A FALLACY?

Many believe that building a better mousetrap is a fallacy, as creating a superior product in itself is not good enough. As a marketer, they need to have a marketing plan and a branding strategy to communicate and influence consumer perceptions to buy the product. The marketers need to focus on not only the product but also consumers, as the consumers are the king and will finally decide on when, where and how to buy and consume the product. Customers are looking for not only the best technology product but also the value it offers while satisfying their need. In 2002, even Dove realized it after extensive research on women's responses in the beauty industry. Most of the women felt that the models which were used to promote the beauty products set up standards which are unattainable for a common or average woman. So rather than looking up to them as aspirational role models, they felt that they were being teased by these size-zero models and of course that the brands were making fun of them. This insight led to Dove's 'Real Beauty' campaign featuring ordinary women and not supermodels. Now, this brand positioning drifted away from Dove's heritage—a promise to take their consumers to a new level of attractiveness. So the mousetrap did not have enough bait to trap the customer. Thus, the brand moved from product attribute to customer point of view. Customers created advertisements to bring forth their idea of real beauty. The point to be noted here is that if you create a superior product with attributes that offer functional benefits, you are soon to be followed by competitors with a better product with more advanced features.

MOVING TOWARDS MINDSHARE BRANDING

Mindshare branding is the most dominant branding paradigm. It uses brand associations in the minds of consumers in terms of awareness, recall, recognition, and loyalty. As we have seen, a better mousetrap strategy positions brands on functional benefits, believing that they are dealing with a rational consumer, whereas mindshare is all about consumers' perception developed through various communication channels and, above all, experience. Most brands across the world have been developing their mindshare strategies on abstract terms such as 'fun', 'youthfulness', 'safety', 'security' and 'love', and by doing this they try to focus on the benefits that will add value to the consumers' life. Marketers believe that consumers find value in such abstractions and it's easy to understand, measure and manage.

The concepts do not exist as independent entities; rather, it's a cultural expression of what consumers buy, experience and value in a brand. More than fun, consumers experience a particular expression of fun—for example, dancing around the house to a favourite tune on one's iPod. An iPod's version of fun is different from Fanta's version of fun, which is different from Kellogg's Chocos's version of fun. Each brand's 'fun' comes to life as a full-blown cultural expression.

So how to gain mindshare? Al Ries and Jack Trout have answered this when they first coined the term 'positioning' in 1969 in the article 'Positioning Is a Game People Play in Today's Me-Too Marketplace'. Later on, they went on writing a book *Positioning: The Battle for Your Minds*, where they went on defining the term as follows: 'Positioning is what you do to the mind of the prospect. Put another way, it's how you differentiate yourself in the mind of your prospect.' So in other words, you need to differentiate your brand in the mind of the consumers to gain a share of their minds. It's nothing new you do but manipulate the existing information in consumers' minds and form a construct for your brand through positioning. A good positioning example could be that when a consumer is thirsty and the category they are looking for to quench that thirst is sparkling water drink (sodas), the first choice which comes to their mind is Pepsi. This means that Pepsi enjoys the maximum mindshare in that consumer's mind and becomes the top of mind recall when the need arises. So to position your brand in the mind of consumers, you first need to understand what is in their mind, how brands are placed in different categories and how brands are ranked in those categories. Ries and Trout believe that for each category, there is an imagery ladder in the consumers' mind and each step on that ladder is a brand. Generally, each ladder has three–seven steps, which means that most of the consumers have at least three brands in every category to choose from and when that category need arises, they pick up the one which is on the top of the ladder then. So if a consumer has Sony, LG and Samsung television brands on their television category ladder (in that order), then they will choose Sony TV, as it is on the top of the ladder. Now, this is simple to understand but do consumers have such a linear choice structure? The one limitation of this laddering brand positioning is that it does not tell us how many variables a consumer utilizes to put a brand on the top of the ladder. Since the positioning of a brand is relative to its competitor brand, another technique which is popular in use is 'perceptual mapping'. The main premise of this technique is to assume that the consumer mind is like a grid and each brand belonging to a particular category, say cars, is placed on the two-dimensional grid based on where it is positioned vis-à-vis two variables on that grid. So the assumption is that consumers plot a brand vis-à-vis its competition on a grid which has two variables, one on X-axis and the other on Y-axis. For example, a car perceptual map could be measured between two variables, say performance on X-axis and luxury on Y-axis. Each brand, let's assume three–seven in number, is placed by the consumer on that imaginary grid in their mind. Now to understand which brand is placed where, a five–seven point scale can be used and the consumer can be asked to plot it on a real grid consisting of these two variables on the X- and Y-axes.

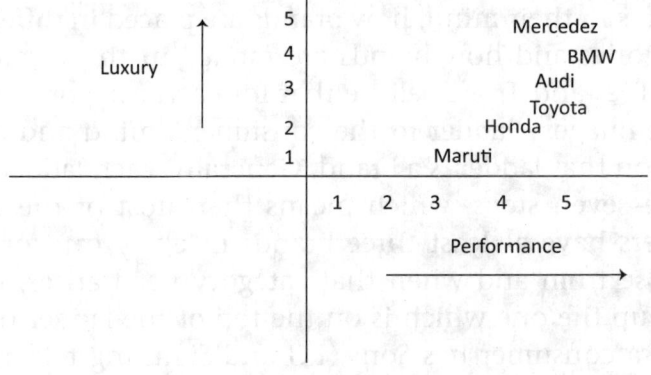

Sometimes the positioning strategies can also go wrong! A relevant example in this is the Tata Nano car positioning strategy of being a 'cheap car'. In 2007, Tata disclosed its plan to launch a 'people's car' targeted to the middle class with the world's smallest and fuel-efficient car at an affordable price (₹1 lakh, about $2,200, with the prevalent exchange rate). This price was between a two-wheeler cost and an entry-level car cost and positioned as the 'world's cheapest car'. Planned to produce 350,000 cars at its Singur plant in West Bengal, Tata Nano was launched in three variants—Nano, Nano CX and Nano LX. Although the idea and the engineering innovation were up to mark, it was not clear at all that who is the target audience for this so-called 'people's car'. Is it for the one who wants to upgrade from two-wheelers or to those who want a second small city car or to those who wanted a Beetle-like trendier younger car? Tata's problem was that they had a noble intention based on market sense, but they could not manage the perceptions of the people and failed on the hype which the launch created. Further, a car in India is a prized possession and is looked at as you are moving up the social and economic ladder. But the owners shy away from Nano, as the perception which was built around the car was that of buying a low-priced car because your income cannot afford a bigger car. So the Nano positioning became a disaster and could not live up to people's expectations for whom the car was launched. There are many cases of successful companies going wrong with the positioning of their brands. Ford Motors, in 1957, launched a car named after Henry Ford's son Edsel Ford, and within two years they had to stop its production as the car was overpriced as the car of the future. Another big brand failure was of Coca-Cola in the year 1992, when challenged by Pepsi's sweeter taste, Coca-Cola changed its formulation and called it the 'New Coke', but the American public rejected it, as the earlier one had a nostalgic connection and therefore Coca-Cola relaunched the old one naming it 'Coca-Cola Classic'. Apple's Newton, a personal digital assistance device, was another brand failure, as people found it expensive at $700 price and also that it was poor in reading handwriting. Similarly, Harley Davidson launched its cologne range but was rejected as it did not go well with the brand value of Harley which anyways was not of smelling good. In 1994, Kellogg's launched its cornflakes in the Indian market as a healthy breakfast option, but it was not well received by the Indian con-sumer as they were not used to take light breakfast and also the idea of using cold milk vs hot milk was com-pletely a non-starter.

So to gain consumers' mindshare, brands rely on their USP, a differentiator which gives brands a distinctive positioning in the consumers' mind. But the problem in a highly competitive market is that with one USP, you cannot put an entry barrier to your competition who follows suit and beats you with a better USP.

EMOTIONAL BRANDING CAN BE RISKY TOO

Consumers are not rationally but emotionally connected to brands. They consider them as a friend, pal and amigo and develop an enduring affective bond to the consumer-centric, relational and story-driven approach of the brand's emotional strategy. Taking a cue from the mindshare strategy, emotional branding emerged in the year 1990. Marketers moved ahead from attributes or feature-driven approach to the benefit-driven strategy to establish a clear, consistent and distinctive position based on the benefits in the minds of the consumer. For example, a steel-belted radial tire is a feature, and safety is the benefit. Benefits are the outcome that consumers experience after using the product. So consumers do not buy products because they want to buy them or for a particular feature of the brand, but they buy because they want to find a solution to a problem at hand. You book an Uber not because you want to be chauffeur-driven in a cab but you book it to take you conveniently to your destination and save time and it is hassle-free. Also, you order Domino's pizzas not only because you want to eat pizza alone but also because it saves your time and effort by delivering it in 30 minutes at your doorstep. Many brands have practised emotional branding strategies, including Airtel, Maggi, Apple, Nike, IBM, Havells, Titan, McDonald's and Starbucks. Smart marketers tap into human emotions such as rage, fear, grief, disgust, surprise, anticipation, trust and happiness (Robert Plutchik's psychoevolutionary theory of emotions) and connect with consumers to increase their brand equity.

But when an emotional branding story loses its cultural resonance, it gives way to the creation of doppelganger's brand image. Every brand attempts to develop and circulate a positive emotional branding story around the brand, but sometimes it is at risk of cultural backlash as consumers' backlash and criticism can destroy an otherwise successful brand. Starbucks[6] is a case in point of emerging doppelganger brand image, challenging the perceived authenticity of the brand in the popular culture. Started with 1 store in Seattle, Starbucks grew to have 32,660 stores globally in 2020, with 51 per cent company-owned and 49 per cent franchises like the one we have in India. Sixty-one per cent of these stores are in the United States and China itself. Starbucks is responsible for developing a coffee culture in America and now worldwide, with a revenue of $6.2 billion in 2020 down by 8 per cent from 2019 due to COVID-19 pandemic. Successful brand positioning and emotional branding strategies have made Starbucks an iconic coffee brand globally. The success of Starbucks can be attributed to a particular cultural expression called sophistication. According to Douglas Holt,

> Starbucks success was in large part due to the coherent and compelling 'accessible sophistication' codes used for every consumer touchpoint: the use of whole-bean coffee as a visual retail prop, the Italianized barista language, the sanitized Bohemian-cafe design codes, the appropriation of sustainable production politics for in-store signage, and so on.[7]

But Starbucks has been criticized for many things, including killing the local competition (mom-and-pop coffee

[6] C. J. Thompson, A. Rindfleisch, and Z. Arsel, 'Emotional Branding and the Strategic Value of the Doppelgänger Brand Image', *Journal of Marketing* 70, no. 1 (2006): 50–64.

[7] D. B. Holt, 'Why Do Brands Cause Trouble? A Dialectical Theory of Consumer Culture and Branding', *Journal of Consumer Research* 29, no. 1 (2002): 70–90.

shops), falling short of environmental commitments (their paper cups are not recyclable and may lead to landfill), exploitation of labour (slavery-kind condition in Brazilian Starbuck plantation) and imposing American culture on local markets. The way Starbucks was expanding, a media headline reported that a new Starbucks was going to open in the restroom of another Starbucks.[8] Also, anti-brand activists criticized Starbucks's business practices with many culture jam messages. An anti-brand activist site[9] spread anti-Starbucks meanings, narratives and memes. So emotional branding if not executed well may backfire to a doppelganger brand image. Basically, consumers avoid brands which they don't find living up to their brand promise or their emotional branding does not resonate with their culture and popular belief. Also, consumers may attack brands which are big, as they are more vulnerable to the doppelganger brand imagery.

CULTURAL BRANDING STRATEGIES

As we have seen, most of the branding is based on functional attributes of a brand (mousetrap) or benefit-driven branding (mindshare). Many times, they fail or their brand gets diluted by the introduction of 'me-too' brands. But there are brands such as Starbucks, Airtel, Marlboro, Maggi, Maruti and Dabur, which have sailed through challenging times in their brand life cycle, have survived the competition and changing consumer preferences, and have shone to become iconic brands. Brands need to constantly innovate and resonate with the consumers' culture, whereas emotional branding takes a softer route owning one of the consumers' emotions like

[8] https://www.theonion.com/new-starbucks-opens-in-rest-room-of-existing-starbucks-1819564800

[9] ploys. www2.spacehijackers.org/starbucks

Coca-Cola strives to stand for 'Open Happiness', but don't brands in other categories also do the same? For example, Domino's's 'Khushiyon Ki Home Delivery' and Tata Nano's 'Khushiyon Ki Chaabi', so where is the distinctiveness? Douglas Holt introduced the concept of 'cultural innovation', a concept which is beyond economics, technology or psychology and a move away from the red ocean and owning an 'ideological opportunity' in the blue ocean. Holt established his cultural strategy theory by using Jack Daniel's Tennessee whiskey as a case in point. In the 1960s, cowboy movies with their rural backgrounds were a hit with the Americans, and the heroes of these movies such as Frank Sinatra, Paul Newman and John Wayne had been sipping Jack Daniel's, making it an accidental hit. People loved the traditional masculinity portrait by these cowboys by sipping the American iconic whiskey. Therefore, it is the reactionary cultural strategy that made Jack Daniel's such a successful brand. Similarly, Marlboro's advertising agency Leo Burnett failed many times to get the cowboy imagery right, until they struck an ideological chord with the American reactionary working-class masculinity. Holt's cultural strategy business model suggests that marketers should first analyse the most important cultural expression with the target audience in a particular category of product, then identify what new ideology can disrupt the old one and then reach out to the consumer with a new cultural expression which addresses their ideological opportunity. So is this foolproof? We know what happened to Starbucks and also to Philip Morris, the manufacturer of Marlboro. 'The Truth Campaign' was named by the *Ad Age* magazine as the top advertising campaign of the 21st century, which was to prevent youth from smoking as 1,200 deaths had happened every day due to smoking. Legacy, an American non-profit health organization, launched the 'Body Bags' campaign in front of the Philip Morris office. Research have proved that around 450,000 teens kept away from starting to smoke, and it saved anything between $2 and $5 billion of the US healthcare cost in the first two years alone.[10]

Therefore, it does not matter what branding strategy you adopt. Because if not executed carefully, it may result in consumer backlash and creation of brand doppelganger imagery. Well, big brands need to be more careful, as consumers' expectations are high and their brand promises are continuously under scrutiny by media, anti-brand activists and consumers at large. We have many successful brand strategy examples and also not-so-successful ones. Brands need to understand the cultural ideologies of their target consumers and should remain true to their commitment of adding value to consumers' life through their functional, psychological, emotional and cultural branding strategies. If not, they should be ready to face consumer backlash and cultural jamming of their brand communication.

[10] https://www.tobaccofreekids.org/blog/2015_01_14_legacy

CHAPTER 4

CULTURE JAMMING

Strong brands are more vulnerable to its doppelganger imagery.

Author

The past decade has witnessed how anti-brand activists have used culture jamming as a creative practice for the creation of a brand's doppelganger image. The *Oxford English Dictionary* defines culture jamming as 'The practice of criticizing and subverting advertising and consumerism in the mass media, by methods such as producing advertisements parodying those of global brands.' Culture jamming has many forms of expression; for example, the anti-corruption movement headed by activist Anna Hazare was aimed to introduce the 'Lokpal Bill' to keep a check on the corruption in the Indian government. The anti-corruption movement was a non-violent civil resistance to culture jam the government policies and practices which were leading to corruption, through street demonstrations, roadshows and hunger strikes, and by generating awareness among the Indian public through TV debates, social media activism and extensive media coverage of the protest. The most-debated agenda of this movement was the 2G spectrum scam, which even led to the fall of the Congress government in the 2014 general elections. Naomi Klein has described culture jamming as 'the practice of parodying ads and hijacking billboards to drastically alter their messages.[1] Something not far from the surface of the public psyche is delighted to see the icons of Corporate power subverted and mocked'.

Marketers and branding gurus have constantly worked on promoting brands through mousetrap, mindshare, emotional and cultural branding strategies. Advertising agencies like J. Walter Thompson (JWT), a WPP company, have developed their branding philosophies like 'Thompson Total Branding' to create a distinctive image in the mind of consumers. J. Walter Thompson, who was a marine before becoming an ad man, started his career with Carlton & Smith advertising agency in 1868. Later on, he bought the agency for $500 and named it J. Walter Thompson. The year 1880 saw a rise of big business houses and innovation in science and technology. JWT grabbed the opportunity and decided to have an in-house creative department to create advertising for the businesses. This was a time when George Eastman introduced the world to the first Kodak camera and Thomas Edison created the first commercial grid to bring electricity to New York. JWT is responsible for building many iconic brand communication such as the Prudential Insurance logo (1897), the Rock of Gibraltar, Unilever's Lifebuoy (1902), Ford Motors (1914), Kraft Foods (1922), Nestlé (1923), Lux (1954), De Beers (1969) with its famous tagline 'A Diamond Is Forever', and Pepsi and Nike and many more global brands and award-winning advertising campaigns. But despite being category leaders

---

[1] http://www.microsillons.org/lecturesautourdugraphisme/textes/english/Klein.pdf

with maximum share of voice and mindshare, all big brands are vulnerable to the brand doppelganger imagery as they use their muscle power to create entry barriers for competition and manipulate consumers' emotions through their brand communication and huge media budgets. These brands also believe that they are the custodian of the product category and will use their influence to gain a share of voice and retail spaces and assume that consumers will passively accept their brand communication and claims. Naomi Klein aims the brand bullies in her bestseller *No Logo*. Referring to big brands such as Microsoft, Nike, Walmart and Starbucks, she discusses the backlash these super brands have faced owing to culture jamming.

Microsoft, Starbucks, Maggi, McDonald's, IPL, Donald Trump, Rahul Gandhi and Narendra Modi, all have faced consumer or public backlash by culture jamming by subverting and mocking of corporate and political icons. In 2001, Microsoft was accused by the United States of monopoly practices in the personal computer (PC) market by putting restrictions on PC manufacturers to uninstall Internet Explorer (IE) for any other program. They bundled their Windows operating system with IE to win the browser war, as every PC user had IE installed by default while installing the Windows operating system. According to M. Dery,[2] culture jamming has many forms:

1. Sniping and subvertising

2. Adbusters

3. Media fake news

4. Audio propaganda

[2] M. Dery, *Culture Jamming: Hacking, Slashing, and Sniping in the Empire of Signs* (Vol. 25, Westfield, NJ: Open Media, 1993).

5. Billboard banditry

6. Guerrilla semiotics

7. Postscript from the edge

Nike's aggressive branding of 'Just Do It' using all possible top celebrities from the sporting field was stamping its brand communication on anything coming its way. The overdose of Nike campaigns and the brand promise of 'enhancing performance' got a little far for many thinking individuals. The pressure of performance was not always a hit and clashed with the culture of many and hence backlash of Nike campaign by an anti-brand activist. The anti-brand activist for Nike did not spare any of the brand's misdeeds like sweatshop controversy, etc. Nike's CEO Phil Knight once said, 'There's a flip side to the emotions we generate and the tremendous well of emotions we live off of. Somehow, emotions imply their opposites and at the level, we operate, the reaction is much more than a passing thought.'[3] Marketers have considered consumers as the kings, but when consumers wear the citizen glasses, consumption becomes political.

The history of culture jamming goes way back to the time when activists used to deface the hoardings as an expression of their resistance to the brand's cultural ideology. But it emerged as a modern way of protest only with the start of the radio age. In 1914, Britishers during the First World War were accusing Germans of jamming their wireless signals so that they could not connect with their soldiers and the public. But the high point

---

[3] https://www.exchange4media.com/advertising-news/guest-columnculture-jammingcreating-the-monstrous-brandenstein-a-brand-doppelganger-57487.html

came in the 1990s when a Vancouver-based media group launched *Adbusters* magazine, which is now a website.[4] *Adbusters* spoofed ads, as they believed that brands were toxins to our mind, body and environment. They also started 'Uncommercial', accusing brands responsible for overconsumption, eating disorders and making our trade for more aspirational products all the time. The magazine challenged Nike's controversial CEO with a full-page print advertisement in *The New York Times,* stating 'Phil Knight had a dream. He'd sell shoes. He'd sell dreams. He'd get rich. He'd use sweatshops if he had to. Then along came the new shoe. Plain. Simple. Cheap. Fair. Designed for only one thing. Kicking Phil's ass. The Unswoosher.'[5] Similarly, GAP signed Jack Kerouac, an American novelist of French–Canadian ancestry, for its 'Kerouac Wore Khakhi' advertising campaign. This got a reactionary response from the adjuster and anti-brand activists to make a counterclaim that even Adolf Hitler used to wear khakis, comparing its positioning from 'rugged individuality' to 'genocidal dictatorship'. Many anti-brand activists used culture jamming to sabotage or monkeywrenching the pop culture brands to a sudden halt or at least put speed breakers to slow down the image-building effort of the brand. McDonald's has gone through numerous cultural jam attacks on spreading obesity. Anti-brand activists attacked the brand for its products and the ingredients it used, which was far away from a healthy option for the consumers. McDonald's Chicken McNuggets were pranked as '20 Piece Spongy McCarcasses for 4.99'. McDonald's arch, a symbol of the iconic burger brand, has been on constant attack and put on a burger by anti-brand activists

[4] www.adbusters.org

[5] Marilyn DeLaure and Moritz Fink, eds., *Culture Jamming: Activism and the Art of Cultural Resistance* (New York, NY: NYU Press, 2017).

in an advertisement and captioned as 'McDeath'. Also McDonald's slogan 'I'm Lovin' It' has been mocked, where the 'M' was twisted upside down to a 'W' with the slogan 'Weight, I'm Gainin' It'.

HE WHO LAUGHS LAST LAUGHS BEST!

Brands have been using the humour appeal to amuse consumers and attract their attention towards themselves, but when consumers make fun of brands and their elements, then it is a different story. Consumers poke at brands and make fun of their functional and emotional benefits by making a statement which threatens to destroy the very existence of the brands. They create 'memes' parodying brands in the form of JPEG files, GIFs, MPEG files, etc. So if a parody is positive for the brand, the brand image gets a boost, and it will be happy if it goes viral. Amul, an Indian brand with products ranging from butter to milk to ice creams, cheese to chocolates, and milk powder to beverages, has been spoofing the current issues which affect the day-to-day life of Indian common men and creating their iconic ads. These ads have been well received by the audience and have been enhancing Amul's brand equity with less than 1 per cent budget of Amul's annual turnover. But most of the culture jamming is brought into practice because people resist the brands and culture backtalk to them using their communication. Brands which use the emotional strategy are always at a risk of an attack through culture jamming and the emergence of brand doppelganger imagery. So brand doppelganger imagery, rather than always being a threat to be managed, is also a way to give warning signals to the brand that its emotional branding story is losing its relevance to its target audience. So the brand managers should always be on the lookout for the culture jamming of their brand communication and take corrective measures to manage the brand doppelganger imagery. Strategically, emotional branding is to build strong and emotional bonds with consumers and become an important part of their lives and social network. Emotional branding strategies are adopted by many global brands, including Surf, Maggi, Apple, Nike, IBM, Pepsi, Coca-Cola, McDonald's and Starbucks. Emotional branding develops consumer loyalty beyond reasons. Take for example Apple's Newton, which despite being discontinued by Apple still had a strong following and usage by loyal customers. Starbucks's anti-brand website[6] is dedicated to battle the monstrous brand called Starbucks. A snippet on their website reads,

> Starbucks makes us feel ill. With their carefully chosen subtle (but not too bland) colour scheme, they try to suggest some kind of ethnic liberal charm. Even the background music has been Starbucked, watered-down instrumental versions of Hendrix for example, after all we wouldn't want to offend. The quirky living room sofa's and tables are not so quirky when you realise they are identical to the other thousands of stores. And those thousands of stores, like a plague infesting our high streets, a Mcdonald's for the new media generation. virtually every street corner will soon contain that insipid nippleless mermaid.

---

[6] www2.spacehijackers.org/starbucks

Their attempts at portraying a modern arty cafe culture, with left leanings are just a caked on makeup, for the neo-liberal global capitalist thug that they are. Destroying land with their farming methods and lives with their wages to farmers and workers alike. Most of all we dislike their vermin-like spread, subsidising new stores to outprice and close down local rivals, before turning entire towns and cities that horrid green. Blanding out any local culture or diversity and helping every high street look the same worldwide.[7]

Below are few of its doppelganger images.

Coca-Cola has always been on the radar of the culture jammers for its promotion of capitalism and sugar-based drinks, leading to obesity and diabetes. One of the Coca-Cola advertisements 'Taste the Feeling' came under attack by culture jammers as they felt that the young woman in the ad carrying the Coke bottles with the tagline 'Taste the Feeling' implied gender stereotypes, as if only women could serve and not men. The woman holding the Coca-Cola bottle tray can represent other identities including being lower to a middle class, Latina and heterosexual female. The nicely dressed woman in this ad selling or offering Coca-Cola probably to men was found attractive, desirable and vulnerable

[7] Ibid.

individual. The culture jammer came to action and created a parody advertisement with the same visual but tweaked and replaced the brand headline from 'Taste the Feeling' to a jammed version of the ad, 'Taste What You Desire' and 'Come Buy Me'.

This jammed version of the ad revealed the truth of objectification of women as it is presented by media and films in the society. So the ad landed up showing the woman as a product, as she was not adding anything to the brand story except giving a sexual appeal to the Coca-Cola brand. According to Naomi Klein, 'The most sophisticated culture jams are not stand-alone ad parodies but interceptions-counter-messages that hack into a corporation's method of communication to send a message starkly at odds with the one that was intended.'

The year 1984, besides other political events, also witnessed an accident at the Union Carbide India Limited pesticide and chemical plant in Bhopal, where 40 tons of extremely toxic gas methyl isocyanate leaked late at the night of 2 December. More than 5.5 lakh people were affected by the tragedy, and the death toll was high, leading to the short and long-term effects of the disaster. In this case, a lot of corporate social responsibilities were ignored by Union Carbide, a fully owned subsidiary of Dow Chemical Company, and therefore many protests were witnessed from many quarters. On the 20th anniversary of the tragedy in December 2004, a man appeared on BBC claiming to be an executive of Dow Chemical Company and stated that the company had decided to liquidate its subsidiary Union Carbide and would use that money to compensate the victims. As soon as the news broke, the Dow Chemical Company's stock plunged by 4 per cent. BBC soon realized that this was a hoax performed by Yes Man, an activist organization. Yes Man used media activism as a form of culture jamming to manipulate mainstream mass media messages to disrupt the dominant culture. Yes Man had integrated PR and culture jamming to reach out to the public and disrupt corporate and political communication. They had used satirical strategies of image mimicry and satire to create doppelganger imagery of powerful corporate culture through public debates.

POLITICAL CULTURE JAMMING USED FOR THE GOOD OF PEOPLE!

Political leaders all around the globe have adopted commercial branding techniques and created a larger life image of themselves and their political parties with emotional messaging on nationalism and other politically relevant public issues. But there are a lot of TV programming and YouTubers who jam their continuous brand messaging by parodying and mimicking their style and communication, opening it up for questioning and critique. One of these TV shows is *The Daily Show with Jon Stewart,* where the host presents a funny way to counter the serious brand communication by arguing their very basis of brand messaging. Political leaders are continuously selling the 'American Dream' (Donald Trump, former US president) or 'Achhe Din' (Narendra Modi, Indian PM), hoping to persuade their vote banks and citizens at large to trust their ideologies and policy positions more than their competitors or opposition parties.

But in a healthy democracy where there is freedom of speech and choice, one can disrupt the political messaging by parodying or spoofing it. Daily shows like that of Jon Stewart and many stand-up comedians have been culture jamming political leaders and parties' communication and exposing the underlying intentions in front of the masses. Well, branding is all about building an emotional bond with the consumer, assuming that the consumer is not 'rational' in their preferences or purchase intention as they don't have time to evaluate and compare the brand offers and read the product catalogues, terms and conditions of sale, etc. They are just looking for value for money and a brand which can cover their perceived risk. So it's all about perception, and political leaders and parties very well understand this and adopt these consumer branding and marketing tactics to generate brand loyalty for themselves and their parties. So whether it is BJP or Congress or Republican or Democrat, they all are practising soap-selling strategies to be on the 'top of mind' of their vote banks.

In 2004, Pew Research Center asked people from where they get their daily news.[8] They were surprised to discover that 21 per cent of the respondents aged between 18 and 29 years said that they got their political news from the comedy shows. Not surprisingly that *The Daily Show with Jon Stewart* won the best critique award, beating the CBS and NBC primetime news programming. Many of the culture jamming are in the form of citizen–government protests, as we have seen of lately in India, the United States and other parts of the world. The two most rampant protests in India have been the Shaheen Bagh one, against the Citizenship (Amendment)

[8] https://www.pewresearch.org/journalism/2004/07/12/the-late-night-shows/

Act, National Register of Citizens (NRC) and National Population Register (NPR) and the Indian farmers' protest against three farm Acts which were passed by the Parliament of India in September 2020. Although both the protest have been peaceful, both have culture jammed the government policies as anti-Muslim and anti-farmer. The most trending hashtags were #farmersprotest, #standwithfarmerschallenge, #SpeakUpForFarmers, #iam withfarmers, #kisanektazindabaad, #tractor2twitter and #isupportfarmers. Shaheen Bagh hashtags popular on Instagram, Twitter, Facebook and Tumblr were #shaheen bagh, #india, #nrc, #delhi, #indiaagainstcaa, #jamia, #godi media, #bjp, #jamiamilliaislamia, #kashmir, #amitshah, #sosjnu, #narendramodi, #modi, #nonrc, #boycottgodi media, #ravishkumar, #caa, #covid, #nocaa, #andhbhakt, #congress, #aligarhmuslimuniversity, #jnu, #rejectcaa, #indiaagainstcab, #shaheenbaghprotest and #rejectnrc.

According to *The New York Times,* 'Black Lives Matter' may be the biggest movement in American history. Although the movement started in July 2013 with the hashtag #blacklivesmatter, it gained momentum and international attention with the death of George Floyd by Minneapolis police officer action against the deceased. An estimated 15–26 million people participated in the protest in 2020, and the movement is a coalition of at least 50 groups supporting the interest of black communities in America. According to former US President Barack Obama, 'Change will not come if we wait for some other person or if we wait for some other time. We are the ones we've been waiting for. We are the change that we seek.' Nardini et al. came up with a model of how social movement succeeds.

The Black Lives Matter movement protested the American violence; racist anti-Black state violence witnessed a

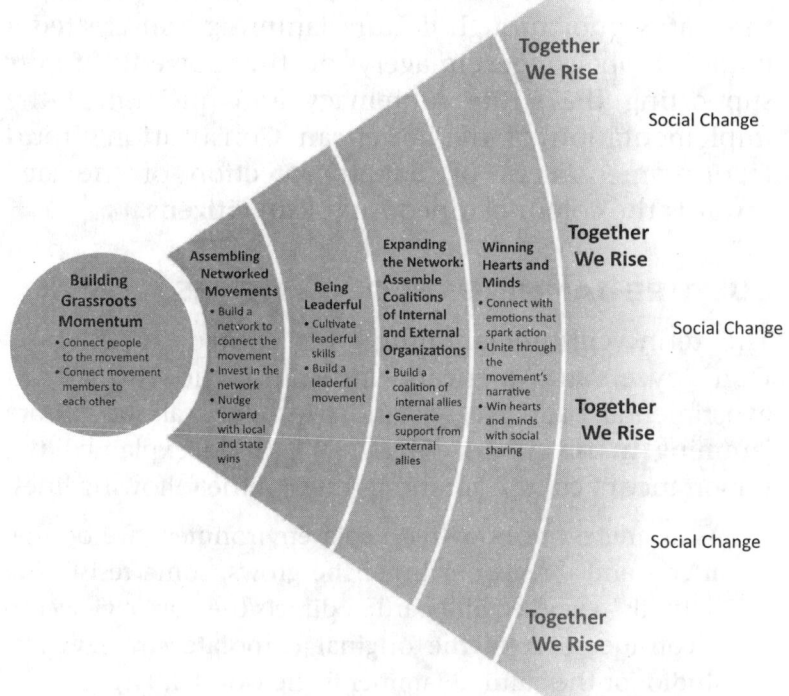

Source: G. Nardini, T. Rank-Christman, M. G. Bublitz, S. N. Cross, and L. A. Peracchio, 'Together We Rise: How Social Movements Succeed'. *Journal of Consumer Psychology* 31, no. 1 (2020). doi:10.1002/jcpy.1201

renewed 'guerrilla semiotics' of culture jamming which has shaken the political foundation of the white capitalist power in America. Besides protest, the movement also used some creative tactics for culture jamming the white dominance and racial discrimination in America. Some of them were using broken 'mirror casket' to symbolize the American police terror; black boys set up makeshift basketball courts in front of historical statues to demonstrate their presence in the American heartland. The hackers jammed the Chicago police radio which was broadcasting rioters news and replaced it with a song by

N.W.A 'Fuck the Police'. The movement disrupted the status quo through culture jamming and created a brand doppelganger imagery of the powerful forces supporting the white supremacy and questioned the implementation of the American Constitution's fourteenth amendment of 'equal protection of the law' towards the colour-skinned American citizens.

CULTURE JAMMING THROUGH MEMES

The term 'culture jamming' was coined in 1984 by Don Joyce, an American musician, who formed an experimental band Negativland. He talked about culture jamming in his album 'JAMCON'84'. He explained the importance of culture jamming through the following lines:

> As awareness of how the media environment we occupy affects and directs our inner life grows, some resist. The skillfully reworked billboard … directs the public viewer to a consideration of the original corporate strategy. The studio for the cultural jammer is the world at large.

Although the idea of culture jamming in those times referred to radio jamming, Ronald Regan, the 40th President of the United States, in his farewell speech said, 'Man is not free unless government is limited.' The 1980s also saw the government taking a back seat to corporates, and corporations gained more political power giving way to corporate advertising, which entered each touchpoint of public space. TV, radio, billboards, airports, newspapers and magazines, you name it and advertising has taken over and changed people from citizens to consumers. Culture jammers took head-on with the brands and 'Absolut Vodka' became 'Absolute Nonsense', 'Starbucks' became 'Starfucks', 'Modi' became 'Feku' and 'Rahul Gandhi' became 'Pappu'. Another tool used by culture jammers is the 'meme'. According to *Collins Dictionary,* a meme is 'an image or video that is spread widely on the internet, often altered by internet users for humorous effect'.

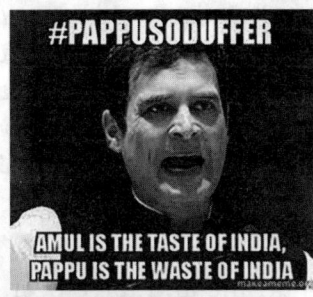

Coke and Pepsi are used as Pesticides in India, because they are cheaper and more effective!

Coke and Pepsi Are Used as Pesticides in India -

Farmers in India in the state of Chhattisgarh use coke and pepsi as pesticides because it's cheaper than pesticides and gets the job done just as well. Video below. Pepsi and Coca-Cola strongly disagree that their products can be used as pesticides...

NATURALCURESNOTMEDICINE.COM

Besides using culture jamming against political leaders and parties, product categories like cigarette manufacturers in the United States have been on constant attacks by tricksters. Besides the Body Bag campaign, Philip Morris had been the favourite of the anti-tobacco lobby. The company's 'Camel' brand of cigarettes and the image of Camel's nose on the cigarette pack were portrayed by culture jammers through memes as 'impotent penis'. Even the cigarette pack warning was named as 'Struggle General's Warning: Blacks and Latinos are the prime scapegoats for illegal drugs and the prime targets for legal ones.' The culture jamming used against the Tobacco industry was so strong that by 1990, cigarette advertising was banned on TV and later on cigarette smoking was banned in public places.

Richard Dawkins in his 1976 book *The Selfish Gene* mentioned 'meme' as a 'unit of cultural transmission, or a unit of imitation'. He further went on stating,

Examples of memes are tunes, ideas, catch-phrases, clothes fashions, ways of making pots or of building arches. Just as genes propagate themselves in the gene pool by leaping from body to body via sperms or eggs, so memes propagate themselves in the meme pool by leaping from brain to brain via a process which, in the broad sense, can be called imitation.[9]

Brands which become larger than life and have been religiously followed by their fans are more vulnerable to the brand doppelganger image through meme as a cultural jamming tool. Fans are connected emotionally to the brand, and any misadventure or misdeed practised by the brand leaves the fans highly disappointed and in many cases angry. Since brand communication no more is one-way communication, the disoriented fan base and anti-brand activists pull up their sleeves and culture jam the brand ideology by circulating comic memes in popular culture through social media. IPL, a global cricketing tournament, is one such brand which has faced public ire for its controversial practices such as match-fixing, money-making machinery, and players' on- and off-field conduct.

The socially empowered consumers and public at large felt cheated by the IPL controversies and expressed their discontent and anger by creating memes, mimicking the issues surrounding the IPL controversies and creating a brand doppelganger imagery of IPL on social media, which was contrary to the IPL's image of a successful premier cricketing league. The IPL controversies (financial irregularities, match- and spot-fixing, players and management conflict of interest, glamour, commercialization of a gentlemen sport, etc.) had given rise to IPL's monstrous doppelganger brand imagery.

[9] Richard Dawkins, *The Selfish Gene* (New York, NY: Oxford University Press, 1976).

Santosh Desai, CEO of Future Brands, said,

> IPL is essentially two things—cricket and entertainment. Going ahead, one has to reduce the distraction around the sport. It is a sports league, and banking too much on entertainment is a very short-term strategy as it fades quickly. You just have to focus on making the cricket entertaining. Adding glamour just doesn't prop up the brand in the long run.[10]

Sport leagues controversies are nothing new. Big leagues such as the National Football League (NFL), National Basketball League (NBL) and English Premier League (EPL) have all been mired in controversies and public backlash. In 2020, Washington Redskins, an American football team, came under controversy because the native American groups questioned the use of 'redskin' in their name and the logo, as they considered it to be a symbol of racism. Major sponsors of the team threatened to withdraw after the native groups culture jammed through protests outside stadiums. As a result, the team changed their name to 'Washington Football Team' till they find a permanent name by 2022.

Even EPL has not been far from scandals and controversies for the last 30 years. Contested by 20 clubs, the Premier League or EPL is the top football league of the world, with each team playing 38 matches and the most-watched league with a potential TV audience of 4.7 billion people. The league generates $2.2 billion through domestic and international TV broadcast rights. On 18 April 2021, 12 of the top clubs—AC Milan, Arsenal FC, Atlético de Madrid, Chelsea FC, FC Barcelona, FC Internazionale Milano, Juventus FC, Liverpool FC, Manchester City, Manchester United, Real Madrid CF and Tottenham Hotspur—confirmed to form a new league: Super League.

---

[10] https://www.business-standard.com/article/management/brand-ipl-comes-under-a-cloud-112060100537_1.html

The new league will have 15 permanent members funded by the American investment bank JPMorgan, with an initial investment of $4.2 billion. The Super League's business model included revenue-sharing and a cap on players' salaries, aiming to generate double the revenue to €4 billion a season as compared to the champion league. The Super League immediately faced public backlash and even Prince William, UK PM Boris Johnson and French President Emmanuel Macron came forward to condemn the Super League formation, which they criticized as a threat to the integrity of the sport and called it driven by money greed.

← **Tweet**

···

Now, more than ever, we must protect the entire football community – from the top level to the grassroots – and the values of competition and fairness at its core.

I share the concerns of fans about the proposed Super League and the damage it risks causing to the game we love. W

💬 1K   ⟲ 9.4K   ♡ 58.8K   ⬆

← **Thread**

···

⚑ United Kingdom government official
Plans for a European Super League would be very damaging for football and we support football authorities in taking action.

They would strike at the heart of the domestic game, and will concern fans across the country. (1/2)

💬 2.9K   ⟲ 10K   ♡ 39.9K   ⬆

···

⚑ United Kingdom government official
The clubs involved must answer to their fans and the wider footballing community before taking any further steps. (2/2)

💬 884   ⟲ 2.6K   ♡ 20.2K   ⬆

With the Union of European Football Associations (UEFA) threat to block the English Super League and ban the clubs for life, many clubs withdrew from the new league, leading to its collapse. The clubs apologized and withdrew their support. Arsenal wrote an open letter to their fans quoting 'made a mistake', adding that they were withdrawing after listening to supporters and the 'wider football community'. Manchester United said that they had 'listened carefully to the reaction from our fans, the UK government, and other key stakeholders', in making their decision.

Marketers and researchers need to understand the importance and impact of memes on any brand and also should devote much of their research to understanding 'memetics'. Brand elements and communication—advertisements, signs, logos, slogans, etc.—are always under threat to be named. Technology access has made the reproduction and circulation of memes faster and effective. Social media such as Facebook, Twitter and WhatsApp have made memes simple enough to execute quickly and cheaply.

With the emergence of the Internet, digital activism through social media has become easier, quicker and effective. Social and anti-brand activists exploit the reach of social sites such as Facebook, Twitter, YouTube and WhatsApp to culture jam the brand, corporate and political messages, and ideologies. These social sites make virality easy, leading to the rapid dissemination of information. Well, can you imagine a world without the Internet? Wherever we go, the first thing we check is Internet connectivity. Even in airlines, we are looking to surf the Web and stay connected with the world. According to statista.com, around 60 per cent of the world population is on the Web, with 4.66 billion active Internet users, and 92.6 per cent access the Internet through their mobile phones.[11] The UAE tops the list

---

[11] https://www.statista.com/statistics/617136/digital-population-worldwide/

with 99 per cent of its population connected to the Internet, whereas China (850 million), India (560 million) and America (313 million) have the maximum number of Internet users due to the sheer population of the first two. The most popular social networking sites are Facebook, YouTube and WhatsApp with 2,740 million, 2,291 million and 2,000 million, active users worldwide, respectively.[12] With the growth of smartphones, social networking sites are now estimated to have 3.6 billion users and will grow as mobile phone penetration increases in developing countries. So with this kind of reach, social networking sites have become a favourite for the social and anti-brand activists and culture jammers. Twitter, as a microblogging site which allows users to post text with a limit of 280 words, has 192 monetizable daily users. As of March 2021, Former US President Barack Obama @barackobama and pop singer Justin Bieber @justinbieber were the most followed celebrities, accounting for 130 million and 114 million followers. With 500 million tweets per day, Twitter is one of the favourite social networking sites for the culture jammers. Many tweets and hashtags have been cultured jammed by anti-brand activists. McDonald's in 2012 launched a campaign on Twitter using #McDstories to invite the public to share their heart-warming stories and experience about McDonald's Happy Meal. But the outcome was the opposite; people used hashtags to post critical and abusive comments using #McDHorrorstories.

 Follow

One time I walked into McDonalds and I could smell Type 2 diabetes floating in the air and I threw up.
#McDStories
8:30 PM - 18 Jan 2012
 135 ★ 35

[12] https://www.statista.com/statistics/227082/countries-with-the-highest-internet-penetration-rate/

···

> What an absolute fucking disgrace! McDonald's tea has gone up by £0.10. What sort of inflation is it in the McDonald's world? #mcdstories
>
> 3:47 PM · Jun 11, 2015 · Twitter for Android

Soon, McDonald's realized their mistake that the crowd-sourced campaign was difficult to control and their social media director, Rick Wion, said to *The Los Angeles Times*, 'As Twitter continues to evolve its platform and engagement opportunities, we're learning from our experiences. Within an hour, we saw that it wasn't going as planned, it was negative enough that we set about a change of course.' McDonald's realized within two hours that the paid Twitter campaign was not helping the brand at all; it was rather creating a McDonald's brand doppelganger imagery. The result was that McDonald's pulled the campaign within two hours of its launch from Twitter.

In March 2021, Burger King launched a Twitter campaign on International Women's Day which led to consumer backlash as the tweet read, 'Women Belong in the Kitchen'. The idea behind it as conveyed in an apology to all the followers was that Burger King wanted to give 'culinary scholarships' to women as they found out that there were only 20 per cent of women as professional chefs.

Besides organized anti-brand activists, brands are culture jammed daily by their consumers who had a bad experience or would be resistant to the tall claims of the brand. Digital marketers should do more social media listening to know in advance when a brand doppelganger imagery is emerging due to culture jamming of the brand on social media through consumer backlash. Tata Group's jewellery brand Tanishq came out with a social media

How stupid can you be? Especially on International Women's Day... #smh

Women belong in the kitchen.

Burger King @
@BurgerKingUK

Women belong in the kitchen

4:01 AM · 3/8/21 · Twitter Web App

162K Retweets 170K Quote Tweets 6

This Tweet has been deleted

Burger King @ @BurgerKingUK · Mar 9
We decided to delete the original tweet after our apology. It was brought to our attention that there were abusive comments in the thread and we don't want to leave the space open for that.
Show this thread

♡   ♡ 2   ♡ 3   ↑

Burger King @ @BurgerKingUK · Mar 9   ...
We hear you. We got our initial tweet wrong and we're sorry. Our aim was to draw attention to the fact that only 20% of professional chefs in UK kitchens are women and to help change that by awarding culinary scholarships. We will do better next time.

♡ 8.3K   ♡ 6.3K   ♡ 30.6K   ↑

Burger King @
@BurgerKingUK   ...

Replying to @BurgerKingUK

We decided to delete the original tweet after our apology. It was brought to our attention that there were abusive comments in the thread and we don't want to leave the space open for that.

4:11 AM · Mar 9, 2021 · Twitter Web App

510 Retweets **1,210** Quote Tweets **18.3K** Likes

...

Replying to @BurgerKingUK
Your original tweet was abusive! It's a commonly known triggering sexist statement that you used to tried to profit off of it as bait. That's why the thread was abusive! Absolutely sickening.

♡ 29   ♡   ♡ 144   ↑

Show replies

campaign to promote its jewellery line 'Ekatvam', which means 'unity'. The 43-second video commercial on social media showed a baby shower organized for a Hindu bride by her Muslim mother-in-law. The campaign received consumer backlash, as Hindu radicals thought that the advertisement was promoting 'Love Jihad', a term used by Hindu radicals for Muslim men converting Hindu women by marriage. Although the advertisement was withdrawn from YouTube, the YouTube description read: 'She is married into a family that loves her like their own child. Only for her, they go out of their way to celebrate an occasion that they usually don't. A beautiful confluence of two different religions, traditions, and cultures.' But the culture jammers thought the other way. Twitter, Facebook and YouTube were flooded with consumer backlash tweets, posts and comments.

Tanishq after seeing the consumer sentiments and backlash to their 'Ekatvam' campaign and also keeping in mind the well-being of their employees and stores rendered an apology.

#boycotttanishq
#bycotttanishq
Should stop one side narrative from liberals and seculars

THIS DIWALI
A TATA PRODUCT
TANISHQ

newssocial.in

NO MORE LOVE JEHAD
NO MORE TANISHQ

💬   🔁 2   ♡ 1   ⬆️

JT
TANISHQ
A **TATA** PRODUCT

The idea behind the Ekatvam campaign
is to celebrate the coming together
of people from different walks of life,
local communities and families during these
challenging times and celebrate the
beauty of oneness.
This film has stimulated divergent and
severe reactions, contrary to its very objective.

We are deeply saddened with the inadvertent
stirring of emotions and withdraw this
film keeping in mind the hurt sentiments and well
being of our employees, partners and store staff.

Although many influencers came for Tanishq's advertisement support, all that went in vain. Marketers are integrating their marketing communication tools where digital marketing is an important component of the communication mix. Brands using digital and social media marketing have successfully engaged their consumers and have built strong brand equity, but the consumer backlash using culture jamming has left many marketers clueless and has disrupted their brand strategies. Consumers today have become very judgemental about brands, as they are in an ongoing comparing mould and do not leave any chance to express their opinion about a brand and criticize to bring them down. So whenever a brand faces backlash on social media, the company needs to decide on one of the three options:

1. Ignore (not find it important enough to respond)

2. Respond (start a healthy dialogue or counter the culture jammers)

3. Delete (too hateful to respond)

Responding to culture jamming is not easy, but brands have been applying strategies which have worked. Bollywood actor Alia Bhatt, who has won so many awards for her acting skills, became the butt of a joke after her rapid-fire round of 'Koffee with Karan'. To the question 'Who is the President of India', she responded with the name of the chief minister of Maharashtra, India. All hell broke loose on social media where culture jammers, the so-called intelligent people, had a hay day launching a smear social media campaign 'Alia Is So Dumb'. The campaign made Alia a laughing stock and #aliaissodumb started making rounds on social media sites—Facebook and Twitter mainly. The campaign was so powerful and viral that it created a database on social media of Alia jokes and you could choose from Alia's 10 best jokes to Alia's 20 funniest moments. Alia took this in her stride and said, 'I look at it in two ways—I'm either relevant or irrelevant. If you're making a joke about me, I'm relevant. So why should I be upset?' After getting bullied on social media and her general knowledge being

Shut Down The Alia Bhatt Jokes. Because No One Will Top Alia Bhatt's Joke On Herself bit.ly/1tAdf8C #AIB

questioned by all, the actress bounced back with a counterstrategy to shut the mouth of the culture jammers with a 'Genius of the Year' video on social media channels. The video garnered 1.6 million views in a day, and the whole film fraternity and even her critics appreciated her take and response on the #aliaissodumb jokes. The video got a big thumbs up by Tweeples, and Alia Bhatt showed that she has a sense of humour and an amazing talent for laughing at herself.

A brand doppelganger image also starts emerging as soon as a brand fails to deliver. Consumers do not spare a brand if they find that the brand promises have not been kept; for example, in 2019, Nike failed to keep its brand promise of enhancing the performance of the athlete in the case of Zion Williamson, an American professional basketball player for the New Orleans Pelicans of the National Basketball Association (NBA). What happened during a highly anticipated matchup between Duke and North Carolina was unbelievable, as the Nike shoe he was wearing split in half while cutting and made him sit on the bench with a knee injury. People took to social media and blamed Nike for this debacle and culture jammed Nike's core positioning of 'Just Do It'. Not only people but even competition joined the party and used this opportunity to malign Nike's image and project their shoe as a better option. The consumer backlash

Wouldn't have happened in the pumas

9:27 PM · 2/20/19 · Twitter for iPhone

1,149 Retweets **2,714** Likes

was so powerful that the Nike shares plunged by 1.8 per cent.

It was a huge embarrassment for Nike and could have been a big product liability case if Zion would have been seriously injured. Bloomberg felt that Nike's dominance in the basketball shoe category was around 90 per cent due to the Nike's Jordan brand, and therefore the damage to Nike won't be too much due to consumer backlash. The Nike crises management team soon came to action and assured us that they were working on identifying the issue and would take corrective measures. After a month, Zion was back playing and wore Nike custom-made shoes for which he thanked Nike and stated that they were incredible shoes. Nike was able to diffuse the creation of brand doppelganger image borne out of consumer backlash and culture jamming of the brand.

...

The shoe fits: The story behind Zion Williamson's new Nike's (Kyrie) after his last ones (Paul George) exploded. Just a casual trip to China and a longstanding Coach K/Nike bromance.

The shoe fits: Zion Williamson's Nike swap pays off in triumphant ret...
After Williamson shot 13-for-13 from the field, dunked five times and finished with 29 points in his return, it wasn't surprising he gave his ...
🔗 sports.yahoo.com

💬 2   ↻ 1   ♡ 5   ⬆️

Brands apply counterstrategies to manage culture jamming and to determine the impact of culture jamming and the strategies adopted by the culture jammers. The brand should first identify the cause in terms of coding and decoding of the brand message, then try to cushion the impact and then respond with appropriate strategic communication. Culture jamming though is a creative practice to express your opinion about a brand but may become dangerous if led to reputation destruction of brand avoidance.

CHAPTER 5

FAKE NEWS

From Donald Trump to Narendra Modi, from propagandas in war to coronavirus, from Mahabharata to Julius Caesar, 'fake news' or fabricated news have been in circulation since mankind can recall. Since then, it has become a powerful tool to spread misinformation and rumours to destroy a brand image and create a brand doppelganger. The popularity of the word 'fake news' is so much that in the year 2017, it became the 'word of the year' in *Collins Dictionary*.[1] Although we would have recently come to know this term, its examples can be traced down throughout ancient history. From ancient Rome to India, fake news has deceived governments, countries, leadership, people and consumers. It has been used for financial manipulations, influencing perceptions, and destroying faith and trust. According to the *Oxford English Dictionary*, 'Many of us seem unable to distinguish fake news from the verified sort. Fake news creates significant public confusion about current events.'

During the Julius Caesar's times, almost 2000 years ago, there was a civil war between Octavian, the adopted son of Julius Caesar, and Mark Anthony, one of Caesar's most trusted commanders. Octavian learned that defeating

---

[1] https://www.thehindu.com/books/fake-news-named-word-of-the-year-2017/article19969519.ece

his opponent would be difficult and that he needed public support to be a successful ruler of the Roman Empire. So he initiated 'fake news' to influence the public against Mark Anthony by spreading rumours about the affairs of Mark Anthony and Cleopatra, the Egyptian queen, and that he was a drunkard. Since there were no newspapers or social media, , the medium Octavian used was to print messages against Mark Anthony on coins. This all resulted in him winning the war and rule the Roman Empire for many years. Well, even his death was influenced by fake news. When Mark Anthony heard the news of Cleopatra's death which was fabricated by Cleopatra herself, he took his own life by stabbing himself with a sword. Later on, Cleopatra also committed suicide. Fake news played a significant role in creating one of the biggest tragedies.

Fake news had created havoc not only in the Roman Empire but also in the Indian story of Mahabharata. The Mahabharata is among the two Sanskrit epics from ancient India along with Ramayana. It is a tale of Kauravas and Pandavas, the two groups of cousins and their battle at Kurukshetra to gain control over the kingdom of Hastinapur. On the 10th day of Mahabharata, Dronacharya, the royal preceptor to the Kauravas and Pandavas, was appointed as the commander of the Pandavas army. Lord Krishna knew that Drona was a great warrior and till he was armed, he was impossible to be defeated. So he made a plan and asked the Pandavas' eldest brother Yudhisthira who was known for speaking only the truth to go and tell Drona that his son died fighting when an elephant named Ashwatthama was actually killed. Yudhisthira did as he was told. Drona, after hearing this, got demoralized and in grief put down his arm. The strategy of fake news worked and allowed Pandavas to behead Guru Drona.

As a neologism, fake news according to *Oxford English Dictionary* means 'false reports of events'. Fake news is fabricated stories which are run in popular media (traditional and online) and is created to influence perceptions of people. They have moved from traditional media such as newspapers, radio and TV to online and have made them quicker and more effective. The interesting thing with fake news is not that they are fabricated but the speed with which they travel and reach households through social media. A fake news can easily claim that Pope Francis endorses Donald Trump or that Hillary Clinton supplied weapons to ISIS. Imagine that these fake news stories garnered 2 million engagements on Facebook, whereas a top story of *The New York Times* could manage only around 400,000. Originally published by WTOE 5 website, Pope Francis and Donald Trump fake news did the rounds on social media, with Facebook counting 960,000 engagements as reported by BuzzFeed, an American Internet media that tracks fake news on digital media.[2] The Pope himself came forward and said, 'I never say a word about electoral campaigns' and called fake news 'sickness'.

YELLOW JOURNALISM AND FAKE NEWS

According to *Time* magazine, fake news is a 'false news [story], often of a sensational nature, created to be widely shared online to generate ad revenue via web traffic or discredit a public figure, political movement, company, etc.'. In the early 18th century, newspapers were a rich man's luxury, as they were expensive and published news for the elites. The year 1860 saw the emergence of printing technology and use of wood pulp paper, which was cheaper than cloth. This brought down the cost of

[2] https://www.cnbc.com/2016/12/30/read-all-about-it-the-biggest-fake-news-stories-of-2016.html

newspapers and magazines and made it more accessible to the masses, and therefore newspapers published news which covered a broad range of issues about the interest of the public at large. The consumption of news increased in America during the American Civil War between 1861 and 1865, caused by seven state unrest against the status of slavery in the United States. It all started, after Abraham Lincoln became the US president in 1860 and the seven states of America—South Carolina, Mississippi, Florida, Alabama, Georgia, Louisiana and Texas—declared their secession from the country to form the confederacy. Besides reshaping the US military, the Civil War also brought out technological changes in the print media to cater to the demand for information in the country. There was always conflict between the military and the press as to what and how should the news be published. Military thought that there was sensitive information that should not go to the public and also the way the news reached the public might not be supported by facts. William Randolph Hearst, an American publisher, once said, 'War makes for great circulation.' Abraham Lincoln realized the potential of the press but was not hesitant to shut down the newspaper which was spreading fake news or leaking sensitive information which could be a threat to the nation. But this may not be possible today, as many websites and social media have become a medium of propagation of fake news with no or little control. According to *Collins Dictionary*, yellow journalism is 'the type of journalism that relies on sensationalism and lurid exaggeration to attract readers'. According to the Michigan State University, without any substantial evidence, the *New York Journal* carried a headline regarding the sinking of USS Maine in Havana Harbor and was considered to be a significant piece of yellow journalism during that time.[3]

[3] http://projects.leadr.msu.edu/imperialistexpansion/exhibits/show/ the-spanish-american-war/yellow-journalism

Both the First and Second World Wars witnessed radio stations been taken over by the military, censorship on photography and newspapers forced to change their editorial ideologies, all done to make the enemy the bad guy and one's country the good guy. Sarah Burns in her book *The Politics of War Powers* said, 'It's understandable that when a country faces an existential threat, it will create a "rally around the flag" effect. The country wants to make the enemy seem as scary as possible and make themselves the good guys.'[4]

From war, fake news has entered our daily life where news is consumed through the Internet and social media and therefore we are at much more risk to consume and share fake news. With news getting bombarded by so many so-called authentic sources, may it be politicians, journalists, celebrities, etc., it has become difficult to differentiate between fake and real. Trustworthiness of media is in question more than ever before. A 38-country research report published on statista.com in February 2020 stated that the level of trust differed across countries. Europe media (Western Europe) was the most trusted one, except for France at the bottom with South Korea. Social media news is considered to be less reliable than radio and TV news. When fake and real are becoming difficult to judge in this post-truth era, people have very few sources to authenticate fake news. Fake news has gripped economies from the United State to India due to technological advancement and penetration, which is helping disseminate fake news faster. India being the second-largest democracy with a population of around 1.3 billion and a low literacy rate makes fake news more dangerous and impactful. Research conducted by BuzzFeed in America found that 75 per cent of

[4] https://reporter.rit.edu:8443/features/war-propaganda-and-misinformation-evolution-fake-news

the adults were fooled by fake news, so you can imagine how many might be fooled in India every day owning to a low literacy rate.[5] News is normally fed through TV, newspapers and social media in India, and a survey of 88 per cent of first-time voters believed that fake news is a real problem in India.[6] With more than 2 billion active users on WhatsApp globally sending 100+ billion messages per day, India has the largest audience with over 400 million WhatsApp users. Considered to be the 'black hole' of fake news,[7] WhatsApp had played a critical role in spreading fake news during the 2019 elections in India. The Indian polity realizes the importance of WhatsApp in reaching people directly and therefore has used it as a vehicle to spread misinformation and propaganda during the elections. In India, the election fever soured high and blended with patriotic flavour during the 2019 elections, which saw people sharing photographs of India's alleged air attack on Pakistan terrorist camps. Although the Indian government claimed that terrorist camps were destroyed during the attack and large scale of damage was done in terms of life and infrastructure on Pakistani soil, but the BBC fact-checker team thought otherwise. BBC formed this team to conduct a reality check on news floating on social media. BBC News Chief James Harding said, 'The BBC can't edit the internet, but we won't stand aside either, we will fact check the most popular outliers on Facebook, Instagram, and other social media.'[8] BBC is working closely with

[5] https://www.forbes.com/sites/niallmccarthy/2016/12/08/report-most-americans-are-fooled-by-fake-news-headlines-infographic/?sh=2cef97db41c1

[6] https://www.statista.com/statistics/1003218/india-fake-news-as-a-problem-among-first-time-voters/

[7] https://www.bbc.com/news/world-asia-india-47797151

[8] https://www.theguardian.com/media/2017/jan/12/bbc-sets-up-team-to-debunk-fake-news

Facebook and other social media sites to conduct a reality check on planted misleading stories masquerading as news. They found out that the photographs doing the round on social media of the 26/2 attack are fake as one of the photos showed a crowd gathered around few bodies but those photos were victims of a suicide attack in Pakistan in 2014. The photo of another destroyed building was from the earthquake in Pakistan in the year 2005. Both BJP and Indian National Congress (INC) have developed 'IT Cells' to influence India's 900 million eligible voters in the 2019 general elections. Both parties have been accused of calling names of the other party leaders such as 'feku' for Narendra Modi and 'Pappu' for Rahul Gandhi and spreading misinformation through social media. Many Facebook pages and Twitter accounts were taken off or suspended, which were linked to either of the party.

Fake news could be disinformation or misinformation; it could be either fake or caused due to human error or reporting bias. In the post-truth era, fake news can be categorized into the following:

1. **Satire or parody:** Stories which are created to culture jam or memes just for fun sites such as the *Charlie Hebdo*-published satire on the latest issues of public interest

2. **Misinformation:** Selective news coverage of a real event to influence the perception of the reader or audience in one direction

3. **Biased reporting**: Agenda-based reporting where the facts are not verified or ignored to support a certain position or view

4. **Clickbait:** Misleading headlines to attract eyeballs in digital space to make money or entice the user to click and visit a particular website or landing page

5. **Propagandas:** Stories not based on facts, which are circulated in the popular culture to defame a brand or show a brand in correct light

News reporting or consumption has always been demanding some kind of sensation which titillates our emotions (happy, sad, fear, surprised and, the new one, hate). Like entertainment, sensationalizing the news sells and news has become stories like soap operas wrapped with some of the other emotional drama. Media, by its business design, also has to earn money and that they can get only if more and more people will watch their news channel or website, as it brings them more TV rating points (TRPs).

When Rupert Murdoch started building his media empire in the year 1952, little was known that he will become a media mogul, owning *The Sunday Times*, *The Mirror*, *The New York Post* and *The Wall Street Journal*'s parent company Dow Jones. He also bought the 21st Century Fox Film Corporation and many local stations which he brought under the umbrella name 'Fox Broadcasting Company'. He was once referred to by economists as the inventor of 'modern tabloid' and had changed the face of news and media, focusing on more eye-catching headlines which increased the circulation of newspapers and gained more TRPs for the TV channel. He focused on stories which create controversy and scandals and would make it more interesting for consumption for the daily newsreader. Today, according to statista.com,[9] the least trusted media organization in the United States is Fox News, where 51 per cent of respondents believed that they do not trust the accuracy of the news broadcasted by Fox News. So changing the editorial policy of the news channel can lead to sensationalizing of news, making it

[9] https://www.statista.com/statistics/255891/trust-in-types-of-news-media-in-the-us/#:~:text=Data%20on%20trust%20in%20various,they%20get%20from%20the%20network

closer to fiction than reality. Editorial policies have not only been changed over some time in the United States alone, but even in India, *The Times of India* story if not the same has moved away from investigative journalism and has changed the way we present and consume news.

In the 1990s, Samir Jain, the current vice-chairman of Bennett, Coleman and Company Limited, the parent company of *The Times of India* and other leading business and vernacular newspapers, marketed the newspaper as any other product. It all started when in the late 1980s *The Times of India* hosted a party where Union Minister Krishna Kumar was honoured. The party was hosted by *The Times of India*'s owners, and there Mr Krishna Kumar pulled a chair for *The Times of India* editor Mr Girilal Jain. Samir Jain was standing close by and felt bad with this gesture of the Union minister. He told one of the journalists that since *The Times of India* had hosted the party and since he was the owner, so why not he be given more respect than the editor of the newspaper. This changed the history. Samir Jain decided to dilute the editor's role and took charge of everything and became the supreme decision-making authority. To make a statement that he was more superior than the editor, he took control of the newspaper operations, even editorial.[10] Shubhrangshu Roy, editor of *Financial Chronicle* once stated,

> In the contest between the publisher and the editor, the publisher wants to be the editor of the newspaper as much as the editor wishes to step into the publisher's role. There is a classic confrontation between the two. But he tried to delink or demystify this. He transcended it. As an observer of journalism, I truly believe that Samir Jain is indeed a quintessential editor.[11]

[10] https://www.mxmindia.com/2013/09/the-toi-story-inside-the-mind-of-samir-jain/

[11] Ibid.

Samir Jain changed the rules of the game and even the industry, as he wanted to run *The Times of India* as a corporate show and the newspaper as any marketing product whose main objective was to make profits. So many new sub-products were introduced within the newspaper such as advertorials and supplements. In those times, people believed what they read in the newspaper and for them to differentiate between news and advertorial came late. So the news was presented the way consumers would consume or need. Therefore, the revenue-generating advertisements started occupying more space than the editorial; in some cases, they even replaced editorial news in the newspaper column. Today, *The Times of India's* revenue from advertisements may very well exceed more than 60 per cent of the total revenue.

When the news has become a marketing product as apparent from Rupert Murdoch and Samir Jain's stories, it very well follows the marketing strategy (read gimmicks) as any product we consume. Whether it is product innovations, penetrating pricing, subscription-based distribution and promotion claims like being the number one in its category, *The Times of India* followed all the rules of the game and even invented many. So as in the marketing of any product, the facts got exaggerated and the battle to gain market share and consumer share of voice and maximizing profits was the sole objective. But this exaggerating or sensationalizing of news reached a new level, where if you can't beat them then destroy them. This led to the emergence of fake news and creation of new narratives to destroy the existing ones by twisting or replacing facts with fiction.

FAKE IT TO MAKE IT!

Whether fake news is here for good or bad, its existence is troublesome. Now it has taken precedence over strategies such as advertising. People prefer to create fake news because of the following reasons:

1. It is more cost-effective than any other way to influence perceptions.

2. Those behind the fake news can keep their identity anonymous and thus can go to any extent in creating and circulating the content.

3. Fake news has a much stronger viral ability as it spreads from user to user.

4. Sharing among users makes it more creditable than a company-sponsored advertisement.

To create fake news, all one needs is clickbaits and their circulation through social media using help of bots or humans to target groups with existing biases, further distorting their perception of reality. But doing this exercise personally is laborious for any company that wants to run a fake news campaign. So there are toolkits available and document guidelines to social media protests. It generates awareness and amplifies the digital protest. It is a road map to take your fake news campaign forward on social media with accuracy, speed and effectiveness. It is defined by The Young Adult Library Services Association as 'a collection of authoritative and adaptable resources for front-line staff that enables them to learn about an issue and identify approaches for addressing them'. Toolkits are talked about in the context of recent social media protests. They came into prominence during the Wall Street protests against economic inequality to inform and mobilize protestors, during the Hong Kong protests of 2019, the climate change protests in 2018 and the Citizenship Amendment Act 2019 and the farmers' protest 2020 in India.

Trend Micro Inc., an American–Japanese multinational cybersecurity software company, has researched the

Internet and has published how much these toolkit services cost if you outsource to a professional agency. Chinese content marketer Xiezuobang charges $30 for an 800-word fake news article. Russian firm SMOService can make a two-minute fake video for YouTube for $621. If you need 2,500 Twitter followers, Quick Follow Now will charge you $25 per follower.[12]

Trend Micro has also estimated the cost of creating a fake event to destroy someone's image on social media. So if you plan to take down a journalist or a celebrity or a politician on social media, these fake news creators can run a negative campaign for a month on Twitter, with each tweet retweeted 50,000 times and negative comments on the posts of the targeted individual for just $55,000. If you need to create a bigger noise with a bigger issue like farmers' protest, it may then cost you around $200,000.[13] Influencing the democratic fabric of a country by influencing voters' perception and choice may cost even more.

Few toolkit cases which came into the limelight were the Disha Ravi's toolkit case and Congress party's toolkit case. India was shaken by the farmers' protest against the three farm Acts passed by the Indian Parliament, and on 3 February 2021 came the Swedish climate activist Greta Thunberg's tweet with a toolkit in support of the farmers' protest. The toolkit justified the farmers' protest and gave some guidelines to be followed by people to promote and mobilize support for the protest through their social media accounts.

---

[12] https://nyintl.net/2017/06/14/2017-06-the-worryingly-low-cost-of-producing-fake-news/

[13] https://documents.trendmicro.com/assets/white_papers/wp-fake-news-machine-how-propagandists-abuse-the-internet.pdf

Listed below are a number of resources that provide more insight on URGENT ACTIONS

1. **Tweet your support to the Indian Farmers.** Use hashtag **#FarmersProtest #StandWithFarmers**

2. **Call/Email any of your govt representatives** and ask them to take action, **Sign online Petitions** and take action to **Divest** from fossil fuel industries.

3. **Organise an on-ground action** near the closest Indian Embassy, Media House or your local Govt. office on **13th/14th February, 2021**. Share pictures on social media using the hashtag **#FarmersProtest #StandWithFarmers**

PRIOR ACTIONS

1. **Share solidarity Photo/Video Message** on social media with hashtags **#FarmersProtest #StandWithFarmers**

2. **Digital Strike: #AskIndiaWhy** Video/Photo Message

3. **Keep tweeting** – Feel free to tag @PMOIndia, @nstomar (Minister of Agriculture & Farmer Welfare), your own heads of state & others who ought to take note, like the IMF, WTO, FAO, World Bank

4. **Read more about the issue** – https://ruralindiaonline. org/en/stories/categories/farming-and-its-crisis/

5. **Physical Actions** – Near Indian Embassies, Govt. offices, Media houses

6. Watch out for (or Join) the **Farmers' March/Parade** (a first of its kind) into Delhi and back to the borders.

7. **Call/Email any of your govt representatives** and ask them to take action, **Sign online Petitions** and take action to **Divest** from fossil fuels.

The toolkit instructed people to

> either find protests happening in your city/state/country and participate in large (or small) numbers or organize one. In addition to the options below, you are encouraged to organize solidarity protests either at/near Indian Embassies, near your local Govt. offices, or offices. Do continue to organize gatherings as and when possible.[14]

The Delhi Police soon started investigating the origin of the toolkit. They contacted Google India and other social media companies to find out the creator of the toolkit. Their effort led them to Disha Ravi, an Indian youth climate change activist, and she was arrested on 14 February 2021 and was charged with sedition and then released on 23 February 2021.[15] After the 22-year-old was released, her press statement was: 'In all the years that someone had asked me where I see myself, I would have never answered jail but here I was.' While hearing her bail plea, the judge said, 'Considering the scanty and sketchy evidence on record, I do not find any palpable reason to breach the rule of bail for a 22-year-old girl who has absolutely no criminal antecedents.' So toolkits could be a tool for mobilizing protests on social media for real or fake reasons, depending on the side of the story you are on. Sometimes it is for genuinely factual reasons and sometimes it may be for fictitious or fake logic created through toolkits to destroy a legitimate or established brand.

---

[14] https://www.jantakareporter.com/india/explained-greta-thunbergs-farmers-toolkit-and-its-criminal-portions-that-led-to-disha-ravis-arrest/331419/

[15] https://www.hindustantimes.com/india/india-news/disha-ravi-shared-google-toolkit-with-greta-thunberg-says-delhi-police-1016133037 96011.html

Fake news is a means to an end, not an end in itself. People who are behind creating fake news or toolkits have a clear goal in mind, and the objective is to mobilize more and more people towards the fulfilment of those objectives and reach the goal. News today is no more a product of investigative journalism (maybe in some cases) but is getting trapped in 'the breaking news' syndrome. Because the media houses are fighting to be the first to break any news, little goes behind checking and verifying the facts deep down. So to some extent, all news can be biased or not backed by the real facts. But fake news is completely based on fabricated news stories with clickbait headlines to get eyeballs. Fake news does not limit itself to creating a fabricated news story, but its success also depends on whom you target and where you circulate it. Users react to different stories differently. One may find one story motivating enough to participate and like, comment or share it among their social network, others may not. Targeting the right audience for circulating fake news can be done easily through the available digital marketing tools. You can target your content by selecting an audience on social media by demographics, etc. But the social media by design is such that people can get addicted to it and the content circulated can manipulate them and can be used to viral conspiracy theories and disinformation among popular culture. Social media has become such a powerful tool in the hands of tech designers that they can influence the perceptions and control over the way we think, act and live our lives. Social media affects our mental health. According to the *American Journal of Epidemiology*, 'A 5,000 person study found that higher social media use correlated with self-reported declines in mental and physical health and life satisfaction.'[16] Social media reach

---

[16] https://www.thesocialdilemma.com/

and its ability to get the message across on an individual profile basis has made it the number one delivery vehicle for all fake news. There are around 4.2 billion active social media users worldwide, which is around 53.6 per cent of the total world's population. With a year-on-year increase of 13 per cent[17] (490 million new users) in 2019, it has the power to influence brand perceptions, start new trends, change the democratic fabric and influence voters' choices. Social media is the favourite playground for the fake news creators and according to *The New York Times* report in 2019, 'The number of countries with political disinformation campaigns on social media has doubled in the past 2 years.'[18] The social media algorithms are influencing users' social media behaviour and tracking every movement of yours through various mathematical models to invade your privacy. So an algorithm is a basic set of rules which a computer follows to achieve its goals, whereas according to *Webster's Dictionary*, a search algorithm 'is a procedure that determines what kind of information is retrieved from a large mass of data'. The social media algorithms are persuasive; they influence our buying behaviour, our consumption even if it's the news and our voting preferences. Known as persuasive technology or persuasive algorithms, it means that the software behind these social media sites is capable of influencing our attitude or behaviour. Russell Crowe made a statement in the movie *The Insider*: 'Cigarettes are a delivery vehicle for nicotine.' Similarly, social media sites are the delivery vehicle for fake news.

Cambridge Analytica did just that. They acquired data of 87 million Facebook active users in America to swing the

---

[17] https://www.statista.com/statistics/617136/digital-population-worldwide/

[18] https://www.nytimes.com/2019/09/26/technology/government-disinformation-cyber-troops.html

US elections.[19] So who is to be blamed, Facebook or Cambridge Analytica? Well, a Facebook user is not even aware that their engagement on the social networking site has given away a lot of their information to a third party, which would be used for profits or changing or influencing consumer behaviour towards a particular brand, political party, economic or social issue. Many Facebook users might not even be aware that their favourite social networking site is letting a third party gather their personal information through quizzes, opinion polls and other engagement content such as:

- Which celebrity was you at your previous birth?
- Or which Hollywood actor do you resemble?
- Or what you might be doing in 2025?

Cambridge Analytica grabbed the opportunity to use data of Facebook users, psychologically profiled, and used it to influence voter choice to swing the 2016 US elections. Christopher Wylie, the ex-Cambridge Analytica data consultant who blew the whistle on Cambridge Analytica's problematic operations, said, 'When you're building an algorithm, you first need to create a training set.'[20] It means that you need to collect data from a sample of Facebook users and gather information through Facebook likes and personality tests using a questionnaire as your research tool to develop a psychological profile of the Facebook user and make predictions of their future behaviour (political orientation). Personality traits of Facebook users were created by asking them to fill a 120-question questionnaire for an

---

[19] https://www.nytimes.com/2018/04/04/technology/mark-zuckerberg-testify-congress.html

[20] https://www.theguardian.com/news/2018/may/06/cambridge-analytica-how-turn-clicks-into-votes-christopher-wylie

amount ranging between \$2 and \$5. These personality traits were based on the OCEAN model (openness, conscientiousness, extraversion, agreeableness and neuroticism), the big five traits of personality. So how Cambridge Analytica[21] gathered 50 million Facebook users' data can be explained in the below figure.

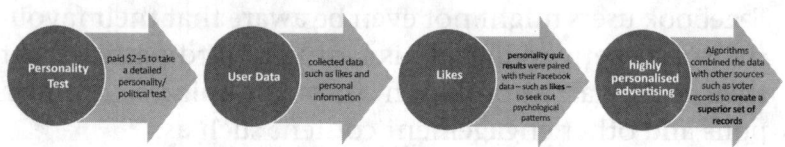

Source: Recreated by the author; https://www.theguardian.com/technology/2018/mar/17/facebook-cambridge-analytica-kogan-data-algorithm

The first thing which the company did was to create an app and pay \$2–\$5 to 32,000 US voters to take a personality test by logging in the app through their Facebook account. Once they logged in through their Facebook account, the company easily collected their personal information and data on likes, interests, etc., and also collected data of their friends on the social networking site. This exercise amounted to the collection of data of 50 million Facebook active users and their friends. The company mapped the Facebook data with the personality test data to draw the psychological profile of the user and the group as a whole by studying the data trends. So after combining the Facebook data with the personality test information, it was then combined with the voter information through an algorithm, and hundreds of data points were created per person to define their personality type. Personalized digital content was then created and

[21] https://www.theguardian.com/news/2018/mar/17/cambridge-analytica-facebook-influence-us-election

targeted towards these personality types individuals. The content was based on a dog-whistle campaign, where the nature of the language was such that it looked like normal communication but intended specific things to the target audience without provoking the opposition. The objective was to garner support for a particular political party and engineer an electoral swing in their favour.

The above is a great example of creating a brand doppelganger image of Hillary Rodham Clinton, the US presidential candidate opposite Donald Trump in 2016. This news painted a doppelganger image of Hillary Clinton as

...

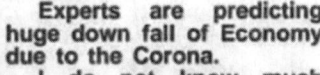

This post has neither been said, nor written by me. I urge you to verify media circulated on WhatsApp and social platforms. If I have something to say, I will say it on my official channels. Hope you are safe and do take care.

Very motivational at this hour
● Ratan Tata

Experts are predicting huge down fall of Economy due to the Corona.

I do not know much about these experts.

But I know for sure that they do not know anything about the value of human motivation and determined efforts.

If experts were to be believed, after the total destruction in 2nd World War Japan had NO future. BUT the same Japan in just 3 decades or so, made US cry at the market place.

If the experts were to be believed, Israel should have been wiped out from the world map by the Arabs, but the fact is different.

a cheat and liar, who couldn't keep America safe, and that she was not with the people of America, resulting in her loss in the 2016 US presidential elections. Fake news can cause irreversible damage to the reputation of a brand, hurt a brand's bottom line, bring down the stock prices and create a PR crisis for the brand. Today, there is hardly any company or a brand which is not facing a fake news onslaught on social media. The more bigger and famous you are, the more vulnerable you are to the brand doppelganger effect created by fake news. Companies' CEOs have recently come out and denied a lot of fake news circulating on popular social media sites. Recently, Ratan Tata, an Indian industrialist, philanthropist and former chairman of Tata Sons, came out on Twitter denying fake news on predicting a huge fall out of the Indian economy due to COVID-19.

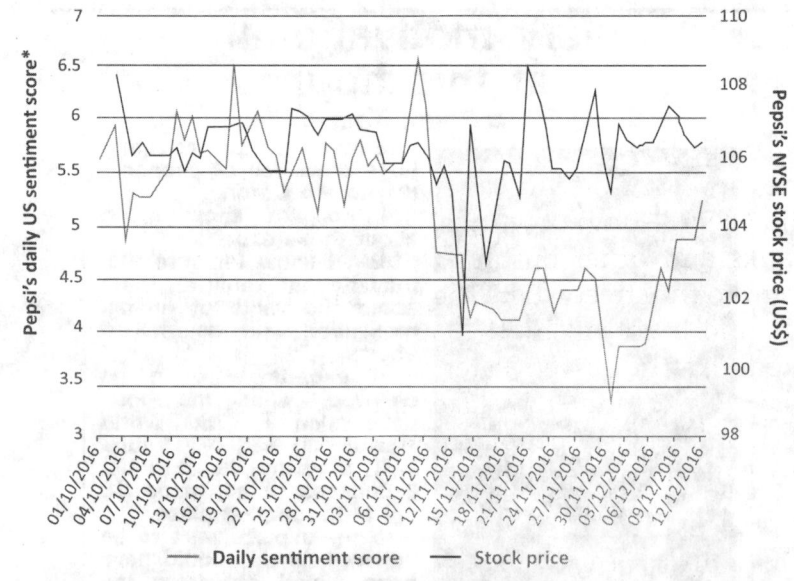

Source: https://money.cnn.com/2016/11/16/news/companies/pepsi-fake-news-boycott-trump/

Troll Proof Branding in the Age of Doppelgangers

In 2016, fake news was in great circulation, thanks to the US presidential elections, but other brands also suffered from this monstrous weapon of brand destruction. In the same year, Pepsi faced a fake news attack by Trump supporters on a quote that Pepsi CEO Indra Nooyi never made. The moment the fake news went viral and the social media text data started showing negative sentiments towards Pepsi, its impact was seen on the New York Stock Exchange.[22]

The above sentiment analysis of Pepsi on social media clearly shows a dip in sentiment and its impact on Pepsi stock from 15 November 2016 onwards. Although the sentiments recovered within five days, the stock prices took almost three months to recover. With fake news, the biggest factor which contributes to its success and impact is amplification. Amplification of fake news on social media provides confirmation bias and increases its credibility of being close to the truth. The more and more people see fake news, they after some time start believing it. Not only new brands but high technology brands like Tesla were attacked by fake news. On 8 January 2019, at the Consumer Electronics Show (CES), a Tesla car was believed to have hit a robot called Promobot while a potential customer was test driving the car on self-driving mode. The robot was on display at the CES to show how it could work as a host in hotels, banks and other business establishments.[23] The robot went to the street where the test drive for Tesla was going on, and it got hit by the car driven on the self-driving mode by the driver. Later, it was figured out that the news was completely fake and was created to shake the confidence of people in self-driven cars and bring the stock of companies like Tesla down. There are many such

[22] https://money.cnn.com/2016/11/16/news/companies/pepsi-fake-news-boycott-trump/

[23] https://www.archpaper.com/2019/01/tesla-killed-robot-ces/

examples where fake news was created to destroy brands and shake consumer confidence in them.

HOW SOCIAL MEDIA COMPANIES ARE COMBATING FAKE NEWS

Post the Cambridge Analytica scandal, Mark Zuckerberg had to face the US Congress to explain his company's stand and role in the data-sharing scandal. It was a five-hour long meeting with the US Senate, where questions were thrown at the Facebook chief on privacy, data mining and regulations.[24] The public confidence in social media is all-time low regarding these issues, and they are worried about getting watched all the time, with fear of personal data getting stolen, and what to believe and what not to. This has led to many people taking social media detox as it started affecting their mental health. According to Mark Zuckerberg, the founder of Facebook, there are three kinds of fake news. First is the fake news created by spammers, which he thinks is much easy to deal with. Secondly is the one created by the State like the Russian bots, which he believes can be identified and removed as fake accounts. The third and the most difficult category he feels is the fake news from the real media with varying levels of accuracy and trustworthiness. A lot of efforts have been made by social networking sites to curb the fake news.

- Facebook is doing third-party checking of fake news and trying to stop its spread to limit the economic incentives of the spammers
- Changes in policies to stop fake news postings

[24] https://www.indiatoday.in/technology/news/story/facebook-ceo-mark-zuckerberg-testifies-before-us-senate-for-5-hours-everything-important-1209448-2018-04-11

Troll Proof Branding in the Age of Doppelgangers

- Identifying and deleting spam accounts by applying machine learning
- Identifying and deleting fake accounts

To not become arbiters of truth, Facebook has developed some products to counter fake news, including newsfeed ranking improvement, easier reporting of fake news and working with independent fact-checking organizations. Further, Facebook is educating people so that they can make more informed decisions about how to identify a real story from fake and on sharing what and what not. For this, Facebook is working with journalists and organizations to launch a literacy project for people to be more informed and smart consumers of news on social media.

Twitter is going to have rules and policies to fight fake news. Their general policies cover sensitive media, hateful conduct, child sexual exploitation, impersonation and many more. Twitter has developed a new policy to fight false and misleading information about COVID-19 such as the persistent conspiracy theories, information not backed by research and spreading rumours, which may lead people not to make informed decisions and may put themselves, their families and the community at large on risk. The policy divided the fake news about COVID-19 into five categories and announced to label or remove such posts.[25]

1. False or misleading information about the nature of the virus
2. False or misleading information about the efficacy and/or safety of preventative measures, treatments or other precautions to mitigate or treat the disease

3. False or misleading information about official regulations, restrictions or exemptions about health advisories

4. False or misleading information about the prevalence of the virus or risk of infection or death

5. False or misleading affiliation

WHAT IS FAKE OR REAL?

Fake news tampers with our ability to make an informed decision, and therefore we need to have a sense of media literacy to filter what is real or fake. Most people now consume news through social media, particularly the youngsters, and if youngsters are the future, the future might be ill-informed. Well, today these youngsters called the 'digital natives' are juggling their lives between WhatsApp, Facebook and other social networking sites, and most of the time they are fooled by the fake news. Earlier we used to refer to subject experts, professors, parents and publishers for confirming what we are consuming, but in this unregulated digital world, one fake news would be confirming another. Michael P. Lynch in his article in *The New York Times*, 'Googling Is Believing: Trumping the Informed Citizen', said, 'both the world's best fact-checker and the world's best bias confirmer—often at the same time'.[26] Stanford researchers found out that many youngsters cannot differentiate between ads and articles, take photographs at face value, differentiate between real and fake news, and identify a dog-whistle campaign. Therefore, it becomes essential for us to differentiate between what is real and fake circulating on social media. Alexios Mantzarlis, a fact-checking professional, and Melissa Zimdars, a faculty of

[26] https://opinionator.blogs.nytimes.com/2016/03/09/googling-is-believing-trumping-the-informed-citizen/

communication and media, agreed on best practices which people can use while consuming content on the Internet. These are as follows:

1. Check the domain and URL. Look for spelling mistakes in the company name or the domain. If it is not a .com or .co, and is something else, than beware.

2. Check for other sources for the same story and believe if you find the same story through some authentic source.

3. Look for evidence that proves the story such as quotes and expert opinion.

4. Check for balance of viewpoint in the story and not that it is biased favouring one side only.

5. Don't go for clickbait headlines or luring photographs. Verify them by revere searching through Google reverse image search.

Fake news is a creator of brand doppelganger, as the sole objective of fake news is to create imagery, in most cases negative, for a particular brand, created by a spammer, state or mainline media using fake photos, text, stories, toolkits, etc., and amplified through social media groups, forums, bots and social media influencers to destroy a brand reputation. Fake news is responsible for destroying the reputation of many big brands. Brands such as Coca-Cola and Pepsi have also been victims of the fake news onslaught when their products were compared with a toilet cleaner.[27] Fake news doing the rounds also claimed that Kurkure, an Indian corn-based snack food, has plastic in it, and that the new ₹2,000 value currency notes have an inbuilt GPS to locate black-money hoarding. All of them are not backed by any real-time evidence

---

[27] https://www.businessinsider.com/i-tried-cleaning-my-toilet-with-coke-and-it-actually-works-2017-12?IR=T

to prove that these claims made on social media fake news campaigns are real. State and media have been involved in the creation and circulation of fake news too; for example, top US government officials and many top news media were reporting that Iraq has a weapon of mass destruction. George W. Bush, the then president of the United States, said: 'Intelligence gathered by this and other governments leaves no doubt that the Iraq regime continues to possess and conceal some of the most lethal weapons ever devised. This regime has already used weapons of mass destruction against Iraq's neighbors and Iraq's people.'[28] None of the media got the story right and was caught in this game of deception created by the United States. The 'weapon of mass destruction' claim was a huge grotesque journalistic failure, leading to hundreds and thousands dying and impacting many economies in Iraq War.

FAKE NEWS CREATOR OF BRAND DOPPELGANGER

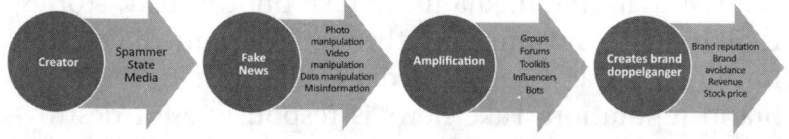

Although many may point a finger at technology and the unregulated Internet and blame the social networking companies such as WhatsApp, Google, Facebook and Twitter for exposing the public to fake news without any warning, the success of amplification of fake news depends on confirmation bias. According to Britannica,[29]

[28] https://www.theguardian.com/world/2003/mar/18/usa.iraq
[29] https://www.britannica.com/science/confirmation-bias

confirmation bias is 'the tendency to process information by looking for, or interpreting, information that is consistent with one's existing beliefs. This biased approach to decision making is largely unintentional and often results in ignoring inconsistent information'. So if an Indian voter who thinks that Narendra Modi is the only option they have to lead India, they will not only seek information to support it but also interpret news stories in a way that upholds their existing ideas.

Scott Adams, the creator of Dilbert comic strips and author of *Win Bigly*, says, 'We are not rational even 10% of the time. When it comes to our beliefs, perceptions, and actions, we are driven by "irrational behavior."'[30] Cognitive dissonance in the consumer mind is created due to the gap between rational and irrational. The creators of fake news create this gap and target people to believe that what they see on social media is true.

Scott Adam advises that 'If you want to see the world more clearly, avoid joining a tribe. But if you are going to war, leave your clear thinking behind and join a tribe.'

Chapter 5: Fake News

[30] http://www.businessworld.in/article/Fake-News-Is-A-Creator-Of-Doppelg-nger-Brand-Image/05-06-2018-151171/

123

CHAPTER 6

THE PSYCHOLOGY OF INTERNET TROLLS

Anyone can speak Troll. All you have to do is point and grunt.

J. K. Rowling

If you can't beat them, troll them! Internet trolling has not only become a big problem on social media, but it also puts the spanner in the online brand-building activity. Brands and individuals get trolled on social media daily, so if someone puts a post or tweet, the troll gets into the action. Rather than participating in a constructive debate or argument, they respond with the most derogatory, abusive, provocative, insulting and threatening messages. Brands are on social media because their target consumers are there, and therefore to communicate with them, brands need to have a planned social media engagement strategy in place. But all are not your well-wishers on social media. It could also be your dissatisfied consumer, competition, anti-brand activist and social media user at large who just doesn't like you or is just an attention seeker. These trolls will attack your brand-associated leaders, spokespersons, ambassadors, supporters and brand communication.

So who are these trolls?

Troll as a noun is defined by *Cambridge Dictionary* as, 'someone who leaves an intentionally annoying or offensive message on the internet, in order to upset someone or to get attention or cause trouble'. So the trolls' main purpose is to demolish the very cultural ideology of the brand or individual through comments on their posts or tweets. The principle of this trolling is that the longest and loudest voice you have on a particular thread on social media, the better you are heard. Trolling is a kind of Internet flaming or roasting for fun, disrupts the online activity of the brand or individual, or could be to manipulate a political process. Most of these trolls have fake accounts and could be a group, individuals or sponsored trolls. Like in the Senate or Parliament you need to prove your majority to form a government and prevail your political ideology, trolling is also a way of gathering a majority to win an argument using the strength of trolls to prevail their cultural ideological difference and disrupt the original message thread. Brad Redford, an American writer, investigator and sceptic compared trolls to 'bad clown' in his book. According to Redford,

> The troll has it both ways. He is magnificently indifferent to social norms, which he transgresses for the lulz, yet often at the same time a vengeful punisher: both the Joker and Batman. The troll acts 'as a self-appointed cultural critic' in a tradition of clowns and jesters.[1]

Although he thinks that we should not take them seriously, is it so?

THE STRANGE CASE OF RAVISH KUMAR TROLLING

Brothers who troll by sitting in India with calling cards from South Korea, Philippines,

[1] https://www.lrb.co.uk/the-paper/v38/n24/richard-seymour/schadenfreude-with-bite

*Russia, New Zealand, Australia, Benin,
Vietnam, the job you are doing will not take
you anywhere. You also know that you are
the new goon of the new age.*

Ravish Kumar, Indian journalist,
author and media personality

Ravish Kumar is Senior Editor, NDTV, and recipient of the Ramon Magsaysay Award in 2019, which is regarded as the Asian version of the Noble Prize. The citation read,

In electing Ravish Kumar to receive the 2019 Ramon Magsaysay Award, the board of trustees recognizes his unfaltering commitment to a professional, ethical journalism of the highest standards; his moral courage in standing up for truth, integrity, and independence; and his principled belief that it is in giving full and respectful voice to the voiceless, in speaking truth bravely yet soberly to power, that journalism fulfills its noblest aims to advance democracy.[2]

Ravish has been trolled for asking tough questions to the current Indian government, bringing out the truth behind the fake propaganda and discussing real issues in his show 'Primetime with Ravish Kumar' on NDTV. He has been critical of the current set of journalists and the kind of news programming aired by these news channels. News programming has changed for the worse, and news channels present high decibel debates, and media news anchors are conducting media trials through these

[2] https://www.ndtv.com/india-news/ndtvs-ravish-kumar-wins-2019-ramon-magsaysay-award-2079102#:~:text=New%20Delhi%3A,journalism%20of%20the%20highest%20standards%22.&text=%22If%20you%20have%20become%20the,a%20journalist%2C%22%20it%20says

prime time news programming. Their signature styles include verbal hammering, sensational breaking news and speakers contributing to a high-voltage tamasha debate. It all started from the student meeting at the prestigious Jawaharlal Nehru University (JNU), and the news anchor went berserk with branding JNU as anti-national and ranting murderous threats for the anti-nationals and creating gladiators to fight mythical anti-nationals in a virtual bloody arena which came so close to reality. Ravish Kumar, concerned about this new image of prime time journalism and continuous threats to his life he has been receiving on social media, phone, etc., questioned himself, his channel and the entire media fraternity that are we to be blamed for all this anger induced in the public. In February 2016, his prime time shows blackened the screen as a symbol of the dark side of news and questioned the TRP battle among the news channels and now with soap operas. Was it that news channels show what people want to see or people see what news channels show—an egg and chicken story for which no one has an answer.

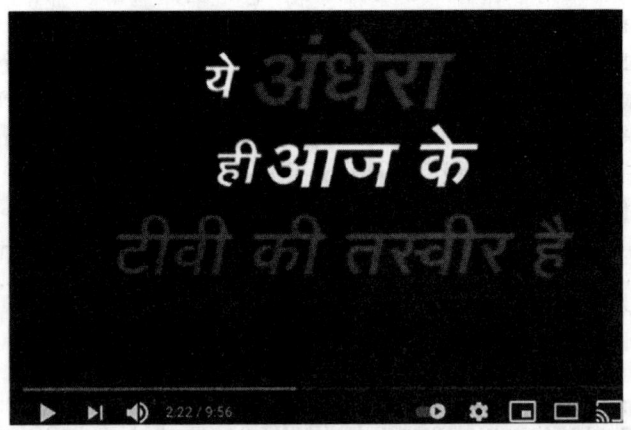

Source: NDTV, '"If We Can't Ask Questions, What Can We Do": Ravish Kumar On NDTV India Ban'. https://www.youtube.com/watch?v= YixrfpeLr2I&ab_channel=NDTV

Troll Proof Branding in the Age of Doppelgangers

One day before, Ravish had covered the JNU news and was trolled with life-threatening messages and calls which gave him the idea to address this issue with a symbolic black screen prime time. In November 2016, NDTV's 'Pathankot news coverage' annoyed the government, and the Ministry of Information and Broadcasting issued a one-day ban on the channel, accusing it of revealing strategic operational details during the Pathankot attack.[3] In one of his programmes, Ravish Kumar became a troll to troll the troll. He got two mime artists to understand what a person in authority would like to be questioned about and how they are governed by the troll.

He then, after being fed up and even scared of trolls who sent him death threats, wrote an open letter to PM Narendra Modi and revealed the identity of those people who were trolling him with death threats. He appealed to the PM: 'To speak in front of power is the courage which has been rightly given by the Constitution and you are the protector of it.'[4] He wanted to bring to the PM's notice that there was systematic trolling done against the journalists who the government considered not friendly to it. Although all of his efforts must not have gone in vain, it is a learning for all of us.

Is there a protection law against trolling?

Trolling is very common on social media and has a global presence. There are no specific laws against trolling in India, as they will prohibit the right to freedom of speech. The victims of trolling can seek redressal under provisions such as criminal intimidation, sexual harassment, defamation, voyeurism, online stalking and obscene

[3] https://thewire.in/government/government-orders-ndtv-india-go-off-air-day-pathankot-reportage

[4] https://thewire.in/culture/ravish-kumar-narendra-modi-social-media-trolls-twitter-death-threat

content. Twitter has come out with features like 'Mute', which will bury tweets from trolls, making them less visible in conversations and search results, even if these individual tweets don't violate Twitter's policies. Also, they are testing a feature which will send a notification to the troll if used offensive language against its target, also using its algorithms to identify these troll and suspend their Twitter accounts. Recently, Bollywood actress Kangana Ranaut's Twitter account was suspended due to a tweet which the company felt was calling for violence and was a violation of the Hateful Conduct policy and Abusive Behaviour Twitter policy.[5]

So the objective of trolls in the case of Ravish Kumar is simply to create a brand doppelganger image of the cele-brated journalist of a media person who is against devel-opment and growth of the country, an anti-national as he is not supporting the government, a presstitute as he is working on behest of the opposition party and so on. The impact of this brand doppelganger is significant on journalists and news channels, as their TRPs fall which negatively impacts their financials due to advertisers' avoidance.

HOW SOCIAL IS SOCIAL MEDIA?

Here's an exclusive insightful interview which I carried with Mr Om Thanvi, a Hindi writer, senior journalist, editor and critic, where he gives us his take on the modern face of the Internet and the trollers trolling increasing humongous with the ongoing surge in the usage of technical devices and developing risk of cybersecurity.

[5] https://indianexpress.com/article/entertainment/bollywood/kangana-ranaut-twitter-account-suspended-7301461/

The conversation begins with Mr Thanvi reminiscing his golden days as the editor of the leading Hindi newspaper Jansatta *and revealing that during those early times, there were active moral policing and the editor was accountable for news' truthfulness and publishing of fake news was considered to be a form of spreading lies. Mr Thanvi discusses his take on social media and how social social media is, where we find him stating that 'There are more anti-social exchanges on social media particularly when it comes to politics.' He thinks that the real truth remains under wraps from the masses because of the sheer amplified sound of the fake news spreaders.*

This can be seen in recent times with the ongoing pandemic and the most relevant example of how many people are even aware of the fact that 'Covishield' is not an India-produced vaccine but a London-based Oxford–AstraZeneca vaccine and is only manufactured locally by the Serum Institute of India and the claims of the Indian government to export two India-made vaccines to other countries as a 'Vaccine Maitri' initiative were a part of an agreement of COVAX between 172 countries. COVAX is a global programme aimed at working with worldwide vaccine manufacturers to deliver countries across the globe with impartial access to safe and effective vaccines, once they are licensed and permitted.

Further, this led to a poster campaign against the Indian PM Narender Modi run by the opposition party. Posters were glued in the Indian capital city and also uploaded and shared on the social media handles of the opposition leaders stating, 'Why did you send our own children's righteous stake of vaccines to other countries?' This was one of the reasons for the shortage of vaccines in India.

Mr Thanvi continues to talk about trolling and quotes that 'Trolling is a new warfare, well technology can be coined as both a boon and a bane at the same time, yet nobody knew that trolling will become such an atrocious weapon on social media.'

When asked about his own experience on trolling, he said, 'Since I am the critic of the current Indian government policies, I deal with regular trolls on social media by those who are paid supporters of the ruling party and their allies. The comments that he receives get personal and dirty as one begins engaging with the trolls.'

To this, he remembers the occurrence of an event when there was a sudden rising tiff in the Rajasthan election, which caused a rift between Ashok Gehlot and Sachin Pilot, and at that time, Mr Thanvi got trolled for his tweet 'on advising the younger congress leader Sachin Pilot that it's not fair to organize road-shows to prove his strength of followers or take a position against his party, still being a state president of the same'. But what Mr Thanvi observed was that the trolls usually belong to a certain section of a caste and therefore sometimes the trolling backfires the troll in the first place as it would have projected an impression that Sachin Pilot is a leader belonging to a certain caste damaging his mass appeal in the state.

On his counterstrategy, he suggested to just ignore or block them and not engage as they are paid to do that but you are not.

DECODING BRAND AND BRAND AMBASSADORS' ROLE

Brands have been using celebrities for ages, and these role models have been transferring their celebrity power and equity to brands. From Tiger Woods to Sourav Ganguly, celebrities have been under the radar of trolls. Celebrity endorsement of a particular brand is a double-edged sword for both the brand and the celebrity. If a brand is caught up in some misdoing, then the celebrity is questioned by the trolls to justify their association or take the responsibility of brand promise and performance gap. As these celebrities are role models for the consumers, many of them buy brands because these have been endorsed by their favourite celebrities. So the consumer gets cheated whenever a brand fails to deliver, and they troll both the brand and the celebrity. When Yuvraj Singh was detected with lung cancer, it damaged the positioning of the brand 'Revital' he endorsed, which is a health supplement, and got trolled. The integrity and stature of celebrities have been in question for long for supporting brands which sell carbonated drinks or junk food which cause obesity and fairness creams which are driven by colourism. Another reason why celebrities get trolled is when they aren't the user of the products they endorse. Does Amitabh Bachchan who endorses Maggi, the instant noodles, eat that, knowing his history of diseases like myasthenia gravis? In India, either appropriate e-consumer laws don't exist or these are not enforced effectively, making brands get away with a lot of exaggerated claims, whereas the US Federal Trade Commission guidelines on endorsements and testimonials in advertising clearly state that 'The advertisement represents that the endorser uses the endorsed product, the endorser must have been a bonafide user of it at the time the endorsement was given.' So when brand ingredients may be a threat to consumer health, should the celebrity be held responsible? Amitabh Bachchan and Madhuri Dixit were trolled and even petitions were filed in an Indian court when a consumer fell sick after eating Nestlé's instant noodle—Maggi.

It was found that Maggi noodles had lead and monosodium glutamate content beyond permissible limits, so not only the brand was sued but the celebrities endorsing it were also questioned.[6]

NOT SO 'HEART-HEALTHY OIL'

When former Indian cricket team captain and president of the Board of Control for Cricket in India, 48-year-old Sourav Ganguly suffered a heart attack in January 2021, it became a nightmare for the brand he endorsed. He was the brand ambassador for the Fortune Rice Bran Health Oil at the time of his heart attack and since the brand was positioned as a 'heart-healthy oil', it was a shock for the consumers and the cricketer's fans.[7] The brand was trolled on social media, and it was a field day for the troll. The brand faced a social media backlash and the brand and the brand ambassador were questioned if they had been truthful to their fans and consumers. Ganguly was a swashbuckling cricketer batsman and an all-rounder who has won many matches for India. He was an inspiring leader and an aggressive captain of the Indian cricket team. He was seen promoting the Fortune Rice Bran Oil in advertisements as a healthy oil for people to have deep-fried food. Although heart attacks can be caused by many factors and not only the oil you use, consumers drew a positive correlation between the Fortune oil and the heart attack and trolled the brand for its fake promise as perceived by the consumers.

[6] https://timesofindia.indiatimes.com/india/maggi-under-regulatory-scanner-for-lead-msg-beyond-permissible-limit/articleshow/47304615.cms#:~:text=According%20to%20Yadav%2C%20test%20results,1%20%25%20of%20the%20fixed%20limit

[7] https://www.businessinsider.in/advertising/brands/article/after-fortune-foods-recent-pr-crisis-after-sourav-gangulys-heart-attack-is-the-brands-latest-print-campaign-enough-to-win-back-its-consumers-trust/articleshow/80928460.cms

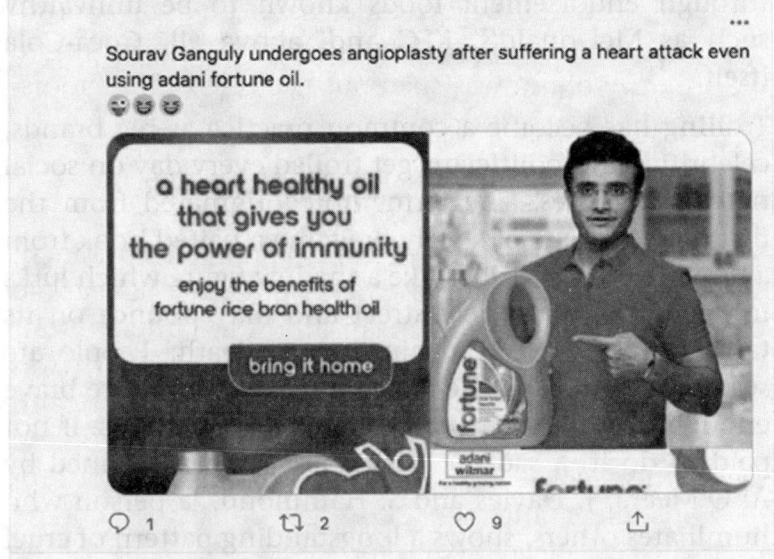

Sourav Ganguly undergoes angioplasty after suffering a heart attack even using adani fortune oil.

a heart healthy oil that gives you the power of immunity

enjoy the benefits of fortune rice bran health oil

bring it home

♡ 1   ↻ 2   ♡ 9   ⬆

The act of removing two Coca-Cola bottles and replacing it with a water bottle during the Euro 2020 pre-match press conference by former brand ambassador of the cola giant Cristiano Ronaldo caused the brand lose $4 billion when its market share dropped down by 1.6 per cent. Not only the Portugal football star removed the Coca-Cola bottles but also suggested that people drink water instead. Both the brand Coca-Cola and Ronaldo who is known to be the fittest sports personality were trolled on Twitter.[8] The gesture of Ronaldo has put Coca-Cola in a tough spot and has created doppelganger imagery of an 'unhealthy drink'. This imagery flamed by the troll has made the cola giant lose brand value from $242 billion to $238 billion. Also, the trolling created the footballer doppelganger of doing 'doublespeak' or 'does not practice what he preaches', as in the past he was promoting

[8] https://timesofindia.indiatimes.com/business/international-business/cristiano-ronaldo-knocks-off-4-billion-from-coca-colas-value/articleshow/83569563.cms

through endorsement foods known to be unhealthy such as McDonald's, KFC and, above all, Coca-Cola itself.

Trolling has become a common practice as big brands, celebrities and politicians get trolled every day on social networking sites. The term 'troll' originated from the fishing technique of slowly dragging a baited hook from a moving boat. A troll is like a shadow figure which lurks in the dark in a lonely street and may pounce on its target and try to beat him/her to death. People are scared to wander in the dark streets, but some are brave enough to walk their path. The troll generally is, if not paid to do it, a sadistic personality and, as defined by A. O'Meara, J. Davies and S. Hammond, 'a person who humiliates others, shows a longstanding pattern of cruel or demeaning behavior to others, or intentionally inflicts physical, sexual, or psychological pain or suffering on others to assert power and dominance or for pleasure and enjoyment'.[9] Trolls are also represented by three personality traits called the 'dark triad'. First, they represent behaviour that of a psychopath, who is morally corrupt, anti-social, manipulative, liar and egoistic and has lack of guilt, no remorse and grandiose sense of self-worth. Second, their personality trait is governed by Machiavellianism, where they keep their self-interest paramount and can go to any extent to manipulate people and situations through deceit and may value money or power more than relationships. Third, a troll personality trait could be that of a narcissist, where the person may have an exaggerated sense of self-importance by putting themselves at the centre of attraction. They are the ones who lack empathy and exploit the

----

[9] A. O'Meara, J. Davies, and S. Hammond, 'The Psychometric Properties and Utility of the Short Sadistic Impulse Scale (SSIS)', *Psychological Assessment* 23, no. 2 (2011): 523.

relationship they are in. According to Jennifer Golbeck, University of Maryland,

> An Internet troll is someone who comes into a discussion and posts comments designed to upset or disrupt the conversation. Often, it seems like there is no real purpose behind their comments except to upset everyone else involved. Trolls will lie, exaggerate, and offend to get a response.[10]

Trolling has evolved over some time from flaming to shitposting to hit-and-run posting to online shaming to cyberbullying. Trolls are mainly anonymous operators and hate their targets so much that they can go to any extent to demean their existence and destroy it. Psychologists think that when a person's identity is anonymous, they can defy any societal norms and engage in acts which they won't do if their identity is known. American social psychologist Leon Festinger called it 'deindividuation'[11] which happens when we are in a movie hall and the light goes out, and people try to whistle, abuse, scream and shout and stop as the lights come back. So an individual takes freedom under a hidden identity and behaves in a manner which is not their public behaviour. Leon believes that deindividuation happens when people are hidden within a group of people like mobs or cannot be easily traced like a fake account on Twitter. Tom Postmes, professor of psychology, Universities of Exeter and Groningen, says, 'Trolls aspire to violence, to the level of trouble they can cause in an environment. They want it to kick off. They want to promote antipathetic emotions of disgust and outrage,

---

[10] https://www.mprnews.org/story/2019/04/24/miller-inside-the-world-of-an-internet-troll

[11] https://www.britannica.com/topic/deindividuation

which morbidly gives them a sense of pleasure.'[12] They are like cricket fans entering a stadium and hooting the opposition team as if they are on a moral vacation. They will react differently if being a part of a crowd than they might do in face-to-face interaction, for example, lynching. In the world of the Internet, such phenomenon is called 'the online disinhibition effect', where a person says a lot of things online but will avoid saying them in face-to-face interaction. Sometimes a person expresses their secret emotions on Facebook like their love for their father which we have never seen them expressing to us ever. The person may express their wishes to travel around the globe or spent their life on an island and also express their inner fears of height or water. All such emotional outburst on the social media is known as 'benign disinhibition'. The other kind of online expression such as hate comments, rude behaviour, expressing anger, and threats on the social media posts and comments is known as 'toxic disinhibition'. John Suler, Department of Psychology, Rider University, New Jersey, came out with six factors based on the permutation and combination of benign, toxic or mixture of both, which results in online disinhibition.

1. **Anonymity (you don't know me):** Well the biggest reason for people to be daring and abuse online is that their social media profiles are anonymous or semi-anonymous. Most of these trolls have a fake identity or an identity which does not tell much about them. There may be an email to create a social media account but even you are aware that how a fake email account can be created on Google mail or other such platforms. The anonymity creates the

---

[12] https://www.theguardian.com/technology/2011/jul/24/internet-anonymity-trolling-tim-adams

disinhibition effect as the troll knows that they can get away with any trolling no matter how much dirty it may be against anyone on social media, though Twitter and other social media sites have devised algorithms to identify such fake accounts or people can use their features to report abusive content and these platforms can suspend these accounts. Twitter and Facebook have suspended millions of such fake accounts and have suspended many accounts which have violated the platforms' code of conduct.

2. **Invisibility (you don't see me):** Sometimes when we are not physically present as in face-to-face interaction, maybe on phone we take the liberty to speak with confidence and are not feared to say anything which in a face-to-face interaction we may not. Similarly, in many online interactions of ours, for example, in a YouTube session and maybe on a Zoom or Microsoft Teams session, many participants if large in number are kept mute, and only they can interact through a chat box or a Q&A. It is very difficult to trace the identity of the person chatting, as the participant may be people the panellists of the organizers do not know. So this gives freedom of expression to the power of n and can be very destructive or disruptive to the whole of the session. The invisibility factor allows the troll to comment in any way, who may even bring up some personal issues or some flashback events which may not show the organizers or panellist in good light. In face-to-face interaction, there is power distance established by age, designations, etc., and even the body language of the other person may restrict your speech or expression. So invisibility like anonymity can be a factor for the production of socially inappropriate comments and/or actions.

3. **Non-real-time communication (see you later):** Many of the most important emails or even employee

terminal letters are issued on Friday evening so that it can dilute the reactions if any in the public domain as it is the weekend and offices are closed for interaction. Since the communication is not happening in real time as you generally will reply to a Friday evening email on Monday morning or if not even on a regular day there will be a time lag, so people enjoy this time gap to write some nasty things as they are not expecting an immediate reaction. This is felt by them as their freedom to write and run. On social media also, this lack of concurrence in time could help the troll to post derogatory comments and run. Further, when online, we are connected to different time zones; this becomes easier, as a troll from India enjoys the benefit of 10.30 hours of lead while trolling and for the United Kingdom it may be a lead of 4.5 hours. So the fear of getting engaged in an online conversation is remote.

4. **It's all in my head:** When people heard the song from the movie *Jawaani* (1984) sung by Asha Bhosle and enacted on screen by the debutant Neelam Kothari (16 years), 'Tu rutha to main ro dungi Sanam', people thought that the playback singer would have been a 16-year-old. Similarly, when you interact with people on social media by comments or posts, you are interacting with text but your mind gives a voice to that text which plays in your mind. This voice is assigned by the image that a person may carry about the other person based on the textual interaction only. Subconsciously, the person may even attach visual imagery of the other person based on their reference from life, movies, comics, etc. These conversations may play in their mind continuously throughout the day; for example, you may have got a nasty email from your boss and the conversation starts playing and you start arguing in your mind

with your boss playing their side of the voice too. So when people do this, they take the liberty to speak their mind out in such a situation which they may not do in face-to-face interaction. This may typically happen online when you see a certain stance taken by an individual or a set of individuals and you paint a picture of them and start interacting keeping that in mind, though when you come face to face with that person in the real time you may have a completely different cues and your behaviour and reactions may be different too for the same set of issues.

5. **It's just a game:** Do you know why people are addicted to the virtual game 'Fortnite'? The answer lies in the compelling fundamentals of game design and human psychology. A Fortnite player is not excited so much with their increasing shooting skills but is excited to get a reward of loot (guns and shields) which is delivered after an unpredictable number of responses known in psychology as a 'variable-ration schedules' like in a lottery, gambling, retail sales, etc. The excitement is that you may get what you want with some reward too. Similarly, in online interactions, people imagine themselves to be part of a virtual gaming set-up where the rules are not governed by social norms and that gives them the freedom to interact in whatsoever manner they may want. This virtual reality behaviour switches off as they switch off their computers and are back in the real world. So a troll is looking for such thrills where one of their five interactions may reward them by winning a social media argument or counter or disrupt someone's post or tweet to make their point on the issue or just to kill the argument by some hateful comments (anti-national, etc.). A troll thinks that it is just a game and will not bear any consequences whatsoever in real life. The extent to which a troll can go can depend on

how much the troll distinguishes between fantasy and social reality. The effect may be amplified when the person is anonymous.

6. **All are equal:** Online disinhibition may minimize the status and authority and reduce the power distance between individuals. I mean you can just stand up to Joe Biden or Narendra Modi and say anything to them no matter how powerful the role or status you have in the social system. You can be just an ordinary fan of Sachin Tendulkar but will not shy away from criticizing him or giving him suggestions on a social media platform, whereas he may be out of reach for you in the offline world. Social media is a level playing field for all, and the person in authority or celebrity status or even brands understand this as an ordinary citizen or consumer can troll and damage their reputation if they don't have a social media strategy in place.

So, does online disinhibition reflect our true self? Well, that may be jumping to a conclusion as our online behaviour is also governed by our personality and cultural references. So a person who is an introvert may find the online behaviour as an effort to break the personality mould, but in many cases, they may remain introvert as that may be due to their acceptance of their personality trait. Sometimes the feelings we suppress about an issue in the real world may get an expression in the virtual events. To conclude that the troll or trolling behaviour is a person's 'true self' will not be a true statement, as it may be just the suppressed part of their personality or feeling that may be getting an opportunity to express online due to the disinhibition effect. So it may be just taking out one mask and wearing another in a true sense as may be in many cases.

TYPES OF TROLLS

All trolls and their attacks are not the same. They differ in intent, purpose and motivation. There are toxic and not so harmful troll attacks. Some trolls may just want to rubbish or make sure that what you have posted is not important enough to be in that space. Some may attack your grammatical errors and some may just want to draw attention to the negative impact of your argument or suggestion. For example, they may react to anything mentioning egg by putting comments like 'Eggs are high on cholesterol' or suggest 'It is better to be a vegetarian'. According to a Scandinavian traditional belief, 'trolls' were ugly monsters who used to hide in caves or under the bridges and attacked anyone who passed by. The Internet troll also hides under your social media handles and comes out and attacks the social media users or their posts. Their attacks are precise and destructive and can take many forms. Some of the types of attack are discussed further.

Shoot the Messenger and Not the Post

Sometimes the troll attacks the person rather than the argument, as they find it difficult to give a counterargument or cannot dismiss it on merit. They will resort to personal attacks, fabricate facts and try to shoot the messenger. So if someone questions the latest petrol price hike, they may be termed by the troll as anti-national, and if they compare the price of petrol with Pakistan, they will ask them to go and settle in Pakistan. So rather than debating the argument of petrol price crossing the ₹100 mark when the crude oil barrel price has come down, the discussion is to shoot the messenger who raised this debate.

Assassinate the Character

People who are popular among women or women themselves, especially if they are independent, famous and

143

speak their mind out, become the favourite target of the trolls, and they spare no arrow in their quiver to assassinate their character. Last year only, radio jockey (RJ) Purkhaa from 98.3 radio FM was the target of trolls.[13] According to her, she just met Dr Shashi Tharoor at the Jaipur Literature Festival and took his interview byte and tested the Hindi language skills of the eloquently famous parliamentarian and posted the video on social media.

Hell broke loose on social media as anonymous and politically motivated users started trolling the politician and the RJ with sexist comments using the pictures from the video. The troll used lewd sexist remarks like 'his new arm candy', 'this time a redhead' and 'his latest victim'. According to RJ Purkhaa, 'The attack was two-fold. I was reduced to my appearance, to an object: a replaceable, expendable entity; because to trolls, it doesn't matter who is sharing the space with Dr. Tharoor as long as it is a woman.' These trolls do not care that the RJ was just doing her duty; they used the opportunity to settle their political scores with Dr Tharoor.

Labelling

The purpose of a troll is to show you in a bad light and categorize and label you as somebody negative whose words should not hold any meaning to the society or the social community at large. They also want people to disassociate with you, as you or your opinion is not approved by the popular culture. They have labelled the Indian PM as 'feku', someone who is a braggart and makes false promises, or Rahul Gandhi as 'Pappu', a small boy in Indian politics who is unintelligent and uninformed.

[13] https://www.thequint.com/my-report/online-trolling-rj-purkhaa-radio-shashi-tharoor

Troll Proof Branding in the Age of Doppelgangers

Many other labels are in popular use such as anti-national, leftist, urban Naxal, radical, liberal and Jihadi.

Women in Bollywood have been constantly trolled the moment they speak up against a particular issue. Jaya Bachchan was trolled when she spoke up against defaming the entire film industry through a series of accusations made against the entertainment industry without any facts behind them and soon she was trolled as 'Jaya Bachchan shameless lady'.[14] Sometimes you can be trolled by people from your industry, and this happened with Urmila Matondkar when she was labelled as a 'soft porn star' for supporting Jaya Bachchan's sentiments, by none other than Bollywood top heroine Kangana Ranaut.

The Critic Troll

These are perpetual haters and will not lose any opportunity to throw insult to offend anyone. A serious type of cyberbully, they will leave no stone unturned to generate a negative response from their targets. They are critical about anything and everything and will try to damage the reputation of their targets through their comments, reviews and opinions. Kamaal Rashid Khan, alias KRK, has become a Twitter celebrity through his movie reviews and is indulged in social media bashing of top Bollywood stars through his trolling. He is famous as a film critic, for all the wrong reasons. He has been dragged in court for commenting on people's films, careers, even how they look, etc.

Sonakshi Sinha, an Indian film actress responded to KRK's sexist post, 'Please RT this if u think @kamaalrkhan is a woman disrespecting waste of space and deserves to be hung upside down and given 4 tight slaps.' Recently,

[14] https://www.mensxp.com/entertainment/bollywood/80537-people-call-jaya-bachchan-a-shameless-lady-on-twitter.html

...

I can't understand why no actress in Bollywood has butt like Kim Kardashian. It's totally disappointing.

9:56 AM · Nov 13, 2014 · Twitter for iPhone

56 Retweets **2** Quote Tweets **40** Likes

♡   ⟲   ♡   ⬆

he has locked horns with superstar Salman Khan on his new movie release *Radhe*. KRK, through his YouTube review of the movie, criticized and labelled Salman Khan as 'Budha' and commented on the age difference between him and his movie heroine. He even went ahead and took the credit for the ₹95 crore loss which the over-the-top (OTT) platform ZEE5 suffered after airing the movie.

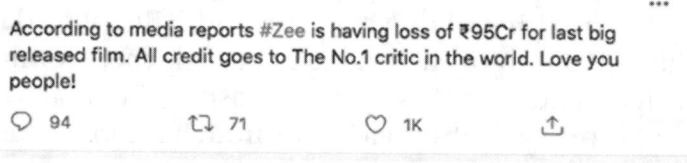

According to media reports #Zee is having loss of ₹95Cr for last big released film. All credit goes to The No.1 critic in the world. Love you people!

♡ 94   ⟲ 71   ♡ 1K   ⬆

Salman Khan filed a defamation case against KRK,[15] for which the critic termed the hero as 'Bollywood ka gunde bhai (Bollywood's goon)'. He added in another tweet, 'This Bollywood Ka Gunda Bhai thinks that he is having fans. What a joke! Abe Tere fans Sirf Mars par Bache Hain, Zameen Par Kahin Nahi Hain! Tu ab apni film Mars par release Kar (Your fans exist only on Mars, not on Earth. Release your films on Mars).'

[15] https://www.india.com/entertainment/bollywood-news-salman-khan-files-defamation-case-against-krk-for-his-radhe-review-latter-tweets-4691732/

Troll Proof Branding in the Age of Doppelgangers

Trolls can be categorized into many other types based on their trolling behaviour: the persistent debate troll, grammar and spell check troll, forever offended troll, blabbermouth troll, exaggeration, off-topic and greedy spammer troll.

HOW TO FIGHT A TROLL

If a company, brand or individual is on social media, they will have to deal with trolls. Brands need to develop guidelines or a response strategy to counter the troll offensives. If they don't, it may spell disaster for the brand. Some of the suggestions listed down can help brands and individuals develop a counterstrategy to tackle trolls and trolling.

If you are on social media such as Facebook, Twitter or even have a blog, you must define a policy for user comments. These policies should define clearly what kind of comments are accepted and what not. Some of these policies are shown below.

Blog Comment Policy

First things first: We love comments and appreciate the time that our readers spend to share ideas and give feedback. Thank you to everyone who comments at the Content Marketing Institute.

However, we also want our comments to be as useful as possible to all of our readers. While we keep 99% of comments, we will remove these:

- Harassing comments: While conversation and the sharing of different ideas is encouraged, all comments need to be respectful towards our contributors and those leaving comments.

- Anonymous comments: We only accept comments from people who identify themselves.

- Promotional comments: If a comment is solely promotional in nature, we well remove it from the site.

We reserve the right to remove any comments from the site; please leave comments that are respectful and useful.

Source: Content Marketing Institute.

HuffPost has also defined their user comment policy on their website which highlights the following[16]:

1. If your comments make this community a less civil and enjoyable place to be, you and your comments may be excluded from it.

2. Comments may be pre-moderated.

3. Be yourself, only yourself, and just one of yourself.

4. Purposefully insulting and hostile language or personal threats are not welcome here.

You can also ignore, block or report the troll. Most of the brands facing online trolling prefer to ignore it, as they feel that not everyone can be their fan. So unless the troll crosses the line of their defined code of conduct, they would not mind listening to them. If it is a celebrity fan or a loyal consumer, it will help the brand to get the right perspective of its online reputation and may also help them to correct its branding strategies (if necessary). Well, a troll has the power to create your brand doppelganger, and brand need to carefully monitor their growth and should have a strategy in place to use this imagery in their favour or counter it through more strategic marketing communication.

[16] https://www.huffpost.com/static/comment-policy

CHAPTER 7

BRAND HACKTIVISM
A Weapon of Brand Destruction

Man is least himself when he talks in his person. Give him a mask and he will tell you the truth.

Oscar Wilde

The main objective of marketing is to make a profit, and the bigger the brand, more the profits. The digital medium has given brands a lot of opportunities to reach out their messages to their target audience through various digital marketing tools and platforms. Not only because the market opportunity has increased but also due to the nature of the digital media the UGC against your brand can be a damaging engagement. Consumers today use all opportunities to show their discontent and anguish if a brand fails to deliver on its promise. It is no longer a one-way communication that brands used to enjoy earlier but a two-way dialogue. Big brands have long been the target of activist groups and consumers. From a demonstration outside corporate offices to a single tweet expressing discontent, the world's biggest brands have been facing consumer backlash on the Internet.

However, the invention of social media has empowered the consumer and public at large and given them a new weapon to damage the reputation of a brand. The companies have always been unprepared to deal with such 'hacktivists' who are staring at their face virtually. Brand hacktivism can surprise brands, as people discontent with the brand may vary in intensity and intentions. Consumers may take up a brand on the Internet on many issues which a brand may cause such as environment (carbon footprints), health (McDonald's obesity), customer service and product quality. Brands are employing more aggressive and riskier branding techniques to create a perceived brand authenticity. Perceived brand authenticity can be referred to as 'The extent to which consumers perceive a brand to be faithful toward itself, true to its consumers, motivated by caring and responsibility, and able to support consumers in being true to themselves'.[1] The earlier branding techniques focused on communicating the brand's value proposition and considered consumers to be passive stakeholders in the process. They believed that consumers could be swayed by exaggerating the brand proposition. Later, advertising agencies started mapping the product attributes with personal characteristics and positioned brands in the mind of the consumer. The brands were the masters and directed consumers as to how they should live their lives with their brand being central to it. From the 1960s onwards, consumers started resisting the control or directives which brands were throwing on them about how they should be living their lives. People could see the commercial intent the brand sponsors had and how they were pushing the brands onto them. Consumers soon realized that the consumption was autonomous and it was them who would decide what to consume and not the marketers. Brands realized this and came down

---

[1] https://blog.revelsystems.com/blog/2018/02/28/brand-authenticity-important

from their ivory towers, as they realized that their branding narratives were reaching the dead end. The marketers learned how to negotiate the consumer resistance to their branding story and made consumers the central part of their story. So earlier consumers looked at brands to guide their lives through products they made, but later this parental guidance faced resistance from consumers in the way of consumer backlash through hacktivism. According to Douglas B. Holt, there are two types of consumer resistance to the brand parental guidance and marketing narratives—reflexive and creative resistance. Reflexive resistance refers to the resistance where the marketers try to dominate the lives of consumers and their consumption patterns through their parental guidance. Marketers build a story and expect the consumer to participate, giving no choice to the consumer. But the consumers who are empowered resist this one-way brand story where they are used as a prop. Creative resistance makes the consumer resist the brand domination and develop their own culture and not get governed by the culture imposed by brands. Also, the consumer resistance emerges from the belief that brands are motivated by profits and not by consumer value, and that the brands give more emphasis to their consumers and less to the non-consumers of their brands. Brand hacktivism originates from this resistance and denying brand domination. A very famous example of this resistance or hacktivism was seen when a consumer hacked the Nike website promotion. Nike offered customers to personalize their shoes with a few words written on the shoe. One customer wanted them to write 'Sweatshop labor' on the shoe and landed up with a heated argument with Nike's customer care which led them to make some logical errors which saw contradiction to the Nike's 'Just Do It' philosophy and their action to censor the customer request. So consumers cannot be fooled by brands distancing themselves from profit-making motives. One of the recent examples is a case in point where brands are projecting themselves as adding 'happiness' to the lives of the consumer. Domino's, Tata Nano, Coca-Cola and many others rode on the happiness plank to make consumers buy their products. But soon customers realized that all these claims were just to dupe them, and the 'happiness' plank became a blind spot and a reason for the consumer not getting swayed by their brand story. So consumers have been showing this resistance through many ways of hacktivism—some hackers break into companies' IT systems to point out security flaws, then there are those who fight for a particular cause and launch anti-brand sites, and then there are some individual consumers or groups who want to culture jam the brand story.

With the growth of the Internet, it is becoming more difficult for companies and brands to monitor, detect and counter the attack by hacktivists. Hacktivism has become the biggest threat for brands and companies on the Internet due to the hacktivists behind it using high-end technological tools, techniques and procedures. Due to the widespread usage of social media, hacktivists can now amplify a single tweet or a Facebook post to demean a brand. One of the decentralized international activist/hacktivist groups, 'Anonymous', originated in 2003, has been carrying out computer hacking, online frauds and Internet stalking.[2] The members of the group are known as 'Anons', and they wear the 'Guy Fawkes mask' during their public appearance.

[2] https://en.wikipedia.org/wiki/Anonymous_(hacker_group)#:~:text=
Anonymous%20is%20a%20decentralized%20international,and%20
the%20Church%20of%20Scientology

Anonymous hacktivism included the United States, Israel, India and other countries; the Islamic State of Iraq and the Levant (ISIL); child pornography sites; copyright protection agencies; and corporations such as PayPal, Mastercard, Visa and Sony. Anons have publicly

George Floyd: Anonymous hackers re-emerge amid US unrest

George Floyd: Anonymous hackers re-emerge amid US unrest
As the US is engulfed in civil unrest, the masked hackers are being credited with new action.
🔗 bbc.com

◯ 391   ⟲ 2K   ♡ 26.3K   ⬆

supported WikiLeaks. Even the Indian hacker group has joined Anonymous against ISIL. Recently, the 'hacktivist' group Anonymous protested the 'death of George Floyd' with social media handle @YourAnonNews.

On 28 May 2020, *Times* reported that an unidentified Anon posted a video on Facebook page wearing Anonymous signature Guy Fawkes mask and threw allegation on the Minneapolis police force of having a track record of violence and crime and threatened to expose them.[3] This followed many attacks on the Minneapolis police website and crashing it temporarily. They also attacked the United Nation's website with its Guy Fawkes mask which read 'Rest In Power, George Floyd!'

The hacktivists who follow the cyberattack method have devised various ways of doing this effectively. These are as follows:

1. **Doxing:** It is the act of exposing and publishing personal information of individuals, companies or government organizations. This can be used to create a doppelganger image of an individual, celebrity, organization or government. The hacktivist does this with an objective to victim sham, take revenge, get publicity, display anger or disagreement or threaten victims. So sometimes you see celebrities getting doxed when people publish their anti-social behaviour or gossip about them in the media. This not only damages their public image but also, if strongly doxed, can bring down their 'Q Score' and hurt them financially. Recently, we have seen KRK giving negative reviews to Salman Khan's latest released movie *Radhe* and shamming him on social media

---

[3] https://www.thehindubusinessline.com/info-tech/hacktivist-group-anonymous-targets-minneapolis-pd-website-in-retaliation-for-george-floyds-death/article31720523.ece

particularly YouTube by calling him old enough and using visual effects (VFX) to make him look in his 20s and romancing the heroine who happens to be much younger to him. Angered with the review, Salman Khan filed a defamation case against KRK. Many of us using social media particularly Facebook or even LinkedIn have encounter people going through our personal information and friend and connection list and sometimes contacting them using our reference. The result is that we use our privacy settings to block them or hide our personal information from the public. In some cases, people even lock their accounts so that no one can access their personal information, post, etc. Doxing is hackers' word for 'document', and it can take cyber-bullying to the next level and ruin someone's career or life. An Ipsos survey revealed that 60 per cent of the parents with children between the age group of 14 and 18 years admitted that their kids had been bullied. In India, 37 per cent of the parents reported that their child had been bullied as compared to 26 per cent in the United States.[4] Hackers can also steal an individual's personal information by hacking various public records such as credit card information, travel records, Aadhaar card information and bank account information to use that against the victim. The hacker may use SQL tools and cross-site scripting (XSS) to capture these personal records. After the 2013 Boston Marathon bombings, Sunil Tripathi was wrongly misidentified as a bombing suspect.[5] He committed suicide following his name being doxed by vigilantes on Reddit.

---

[4] https://www.ipsos.com/sites/default/files/ct/news/documents/2018-06/cyberbullying_june2018.pdf

[5] https://www.nbcnews.com/news/asian-america/wrongly-accused-boston-bombing-sunil-tripathys-story-now-being-told-n373141

2. **DDoS:** Distributed denial of service (DDoS) is a cyberattack where multiple computers are used to generate overwhelming traffic to a particular front-facing site or Internet service, making it crash temporarily or indefinitely. Cisco predicts that the DDoS attack will double from 7.9 million in 2018 to over 15 million in 2023.[6] But it is not the number that the companies are worried about but the use of Botnet, 'a collection of internet-connected devices (Internet of Things [IoT] devices) that move data over a network without requiring human interaction'. With the help of computing, the cloud, big data analytics and mobile technologies, which make physical things such as TVs, kitchen appliances, refrigerators and ACs share and collect data without any human intervention, Botnet is used as a weapon to carry the DDoS attacks. Now even hacktivists can hack the consumer's IoT and can plan a much smarter, bigger and effective DDoS attack. So when the server of a company is down due to a DDoS attack, it may cost them something between $300,000 and $1,000,000 for an hour of website server downtime. Well, Google faced the biggest DDoS attack from China during the US elections in 2020, where their staffers who were covering the Biden and Trump campaign saw phishing attacks on their email to extract the information to the campaign.[7] According to Google's Threat Analysis Group (TAG), 'The Iranian attacker group (APT35) and the Chinese attacker group (APT31) targeted campaign staffers' emails with credential phishing emails and emails containing tracking links. As part

[6] https://www.securityinfowatch.com/cybersecurity/information-security/breach-detection/article/21222912/the-next-new-threat-adversaries-operating-at-scale-with-automation

[7] https://www.news18.com/news/tech/google-faced-the-largest-ddos-attack-seen-yet-from-chinese-state-backed-hackers-in-2017-2974937.html

of our wider tracking of APT31 activity, we've also seen them deploy targeted malware campaigns.' In one instance, the malware was installed secretly on the target user's computer while the user was downloading an impersonated McAfee anti-virus. The matter was reported by Google to the Federal Bureau of Investigation (FBI).

MY NAME IS NIDHI RAZDAN AND I AM NOT A HARVARD PROFESSOR

In November 2019, Nidhi Razdan who was then the executive editor of NDTV, an Indian news media company, was approached for a speaking slot in an event organized by Harvard Kennedy School.[8] The organizers then approached her separately and told her that she could be considered for an associate professor job in the journalism school of Harvard and therefore collected her resume and other required documents for the post. She then was called for a 90-minute online interview by the Harvard faculty and was given the offer of an associate professor position. She also did her reference check about the programme and found out that Harvard has a school that offers Master of Liberal Arts which offered a journalism degree which had 500 faculty and out of that 17 were of journalism. But the alleged human resource person from Harvard kept on delaying her joining due to COVID-19 and meanwhile was extracting bank and personal information from her. So smelling a rat, Nidhi contacted Harvard University and to her utter dismay, there was no record of her appointment with them. Soon she realized that she was under a phishing attack by hacktivists who wanted to extract her personal and bank information to steal money from her. Nidhi had resigned from her job

[8] https://www.ndtv.com/blog/how-i-fell-for-a-phishing-attack-my-story-by-nidhi-razdan-2353395

for this opportunity and was left high and dry as a victim of a phishing attack through hacktivism. All the communication by the hacktivist seemed to be genuine, but actually, they all were fake. So she was left at a point of no return as she had quit her job for the position and was hoping for a second career in Harvard. The lesson one has learned from this case is that hacktivism has become so sophisticated that it can con even a seasoned journalist with 21 years of experience. Second, a lesson for all of us is that dangerous are not those dark and lonely streets, but we can be attacked on the Internet through emails, telephones, videoconferencing and social media. These fraudulent attacks are not limited to Nigerian emails anymore but can come from a very sophisticated source believed to be backed by some great institution like Harvard in this case. So beware! Hacktivism is lurking around your Internet activities.

3. **Defacing the websites:** Defacing a website is an attack in which hacktivists penetrate a website through SEO scams, malware, etc., and replace content on the site with their messages. The defacing will not only be an attack on the reputation of the company but may also bring the business down due to the downtime. There could be many reasons that why it is done—sometimes it is just to show that the hacker group opposes the policies and practices of a company on any social, political or religious issues. Or it could be just for money and may not be an attack on the company but on the software they use. This is a big dollar business with 80,000 cyberattacks per day or over 30 million attacks per year in 2018 alone.[9] According to the *Internet Security Threat Report,*

[9] https://purplesec.us/resources/cyber-security-statistics/#:~:text=In%202018%20there%20were%2080%2C000,and%20health%20records%20left%20unprotected

Troll Proof Branding in the Age of Doppelgangers

February 2019, Volume 4, 1 out of 10 are malicious URLs, and web attacks have increased by 56 per cent from 2018.[10]

4. **Formjacking:** It is an attack using JavaScript code on e-commerce sites to steal payment information and credit or debit card details of the shopper. In 2018, 4,818 unique websites were attacked by formjacking, and a single shopper credit card data was sold in the underground economy for $45 and stolen data from 10 credit cards could earn the hacktivist $2.2 million in 1-month period. The biggest hacktivist group behind this is Magecart, which has attacked some big companies, including British Airways, Ticketmaster, Kitronik—an electronic project kit company—and contact lens seller Vision Direct.

5. **Ransomware:** It is a malware attack which encrypts the victim's files and restores access to the files after getting ransom from the victim. Hacktivists attack those companies which have a weak cybersecurity system or organizations which can pay quickly in cryptocurrency. The process is that the hacker gets access to the organization's computer and encrypts files. The catch is that the files can only be restored with a mathematical key which the hacker has. So if they have to restore the files, they have to get the key in exchange for money. Organizations need to prevent ransomware by installing anti-malware software at frequent intervals of time.

Hacktivism is here to stay and will be a permanent cyberthreat to individuals, groups, governments and

---

[10] https://purplesec.us/resources/cyber-security-statistics/#:~:text=In%202018%20there%20were%2080%2C000,and%20health%20records%20left%20unprotected

corporations worldwide. Hacktivists cannot be underestimated and individuals and organizations have to open their eyes and ears to cyberattacks. Our reputations are at stake, and we need to protect our privacy and technology so that cyber thieves cannot steal our data or jam our networks. Most of these hacktivists are motivated by political and social differences with the victim organizations and not by making money out of hacktivism. That is why they are very unpredictable. Hacktivist groups want to make their hacktivism a PR event, as it may mobilize more support from individuals and groups. The hacktivists leverage this support to amplify and prepare a much stronger attack on individuals and organizations. New hacktivist groups are emerging every day and, inspired by Anonymous, adopt dangerous modus operandi. Hacktivist groups are sponsored by groups like Anonymous, states or individuals who are discontented with companies or brands. So social media listening should be improved by companies so that they can track down the social media sentiments and can devise a counterstrategy for any kind of brand doppelganger imagery getting developed through UGC on social media. Individual hacktivists or consumers who are discontented with brand experience can also damage the reputation of a brand through a single tweet or post. The bigger the brand, the bigger is the attack planned. A brand, if careful, can have firewalls built to counter the hacktivists' cyberattack, but there are other ways brands are targeted.

DOUBLE JEOPARDY: A DISADVANTAGE

In the 1960s, **William McPhee coined the term 'double jeopardy', a phenomenon where brands with a high market share will have more loyal customers and brands with a lower market share will have less brand loyalty. The marketing implication of this theory is that brands with a high market share will use their customer brand loyalty as an entry barrier for new entrants and for competition to gain market share. But it's also true that brands with a high market share will be more vulnerable to attack from the competition, new entrants, substitute products, and anti-brand and anti-consumption groups. So what are the options in front of the opposition to your brand? They can increase their market share by either expanding the market size or eating into the market share of the category leader. The latter is easier than expanding the market. On the other hand, the brand leader will dominate the category decisions such as product, price, place and promotion and also influence the consumption patterns; in other words, they will act as a brand bully. It's also true that you can't influence all the people all the time. There has to be resistance to brand bully, and this sometimes takes the form of anti-brand sites or brand hate sites. If we see, most of the brands that top in terms of brand value have been attacked by these anti-brand sites. Be it Starbucks,[11] Coca-Cola,[12] Domino's[13] or American Express,[14] all have been using their most powerful branding element—their brand name—in the domain name of the anti-brand site.

People start this anti-brand movement by launching a hate website because of a bad experience with the brand or have a cultural difference with the perceived authenticity of the brand. This could be an individual or a group or, in some cases, competition as in the case of Amway alleging that P&G was behind the hate rhetoric about the brand and even went ahead and filed a case in the state of Michigan. Most of these hate sites have come

---

[11] https://www2.spacehijackers.org/starbucks/

[12] http://killercoke.org/

[13] https://ihatedominospizza.wordpress.com/

[14] https://www.amexsux.com/

into existence because some customers of theirs had a bad experience with the product or services and hence launched the hate website out of sheer anger towards the company. For example, the AmEx hate site was launched by John Westphal in 2001, who stated,

> Although I started the site because of a small complaint, now—two years and 20,000-plus postings later—I realize how much more widespread and serious American Express's wrongdoing is. It has led me to realize that I am doing a real public service by alerting the public to the dangers of dealing with Amex.[15]

Many of these hate sites which were created out of anger towards a particular brand seize to exist for reasons best known to them. But brands need to be concerned about the UGC on the Internet. The problem is the gap that occurs between the perceived authenticity of a brand. Consumers believe that a brand will be true to itself and its consumers. When it doesn't, they lose trust in the brand and may avoid the brand or will jump on to social media to talk about their negative feelings about the brand. Consumers want the brand to live up to its brand promise and not try to drift away from it. Zaltman, in his book *How Customers Think: Essential Insights into the Mind of the Market*,[16] mentions that the consumer processes are unconscious more than conscious, and that there is always an interplay between the conscious and unconscious processes of the consumer and the marketer. So whatever brand messages are encoded by marketers may not be decoded in the same way as marketers would perceive. So there will always be a conflict with some consumers, as they may add or delete information based on their unconscious processes. According to Zaltman, memories,

---

[15] https://www.forbes.com/2005/03/07/cx_cw_0308hate.html?sh=3f1ec4c44ed5

[16] Gerald Zaltman, *How Customers Think: Essential Insights into the Mind of the Market* (Boston, MA: Harvard Business Review Press, 2003).

metaphors and stories are all interconnected. He suggests that consumers while purchasing a brand refer to their past, present and future brand consumption experience and then decide if they have to buy or avoid the brand. Well, the power has been shifted from marketers to the consumers, as the empowered digital native can ruin a brand reputation with a single tweet or post on social media. Seth Godin's 'permission marketing' concept may apply to marketers, where they give an option to consumers to allow advertising messages to be received in their inbox. But it does not apply to consumers who exercise their freedom of speech and expression to write a blog, post or tweet or upload a video if unhappy with the brand performance.

'UNITED BREAKS GUITARS': THE POWER OF ONE VOICE IN THE AGE OF SOCIAL MEDIA

Social media complaints have become a nightmare for brands, as very few know how to deal with them with good customer relationship management on social networks. The power exercised by one digitally empowered consumer on United Airlines is one such example of the damage one individual consumer can do to the reputation of a brand. It all happened in the year 2008 or 2009 when the Canadian musician Dave Carroll took a United Airlines flight from Nova Scotia to Nebraska in the United States to perform with his band 'Sons of Maxwell'.[17] He was carrying his Taylor $3,500 guitar with him in the check-in cabin, and when they were catching a connecting flight at Chicago, one of the fellow passengers saw the United Airlines baggage handlers throwing guitars as they were transferring the baggage from one flight to another. Dave could not believe it and

[17] https://www.marketplace.org/2019/07/05/a-broken-guitar-a-youtube-video-and-a-new-era-of-customer-service/

called customer care, where his query was shrugged off. Then after landing in Omaha, Nebraska, he found out that his guitar was broken and for nine months he was in touch with the airline customer service to apologize and pay for the damages. He even found someone to repair the guitar for $1,200 and requested United Airlines staff to pay that amount in flight vouchers. But the airline response was not positive. So when all doors were closed and Dave was left to his device, he created a YouTube song, 'United Breaks Guitars', and it became a sensation with 19 million views on YouTube and financial damage to the airlines worth 10 per cent of its market value, costing shareholders roughly $180 million of stock market loss. Dave became a role model for many musicians whose instruments had been damaged during the airline flights, and they all joined him in his movement for creating a brand doppelganger of the customer service of United Airlines. Dave became famous and has been performing and telling his story in over 30 countries and has received a call from Bob Taylor of Taylor guitar makers offering him to tour their California factory and pick up two Taylor guitars of his choice. Well, later on, the airline gave Dave $1,200 of flight vouchers and also $1,200 in cash, but they could not reverse the damage to their reputation. So 'United Breaks Guitars' was that one digitally empowered consumer voice which could do a lot of damage to the reputation and financials of such a strong brand as the United Airlines.

'United Breaks Guitars' Lyrics by Dave Carroll

I flew United Airlines on my way to Nebraska
The plane departed, Halifax,
connecting in Chicago's 'O'Hare'
While on the ground, a passenger
said from the seat behind me
'My God, they're throwing guitars out there'
The band and I exchanged a look,

best described as terror
At the action on the tarmac,
and knowing whose projectiles these would be
So before I left Chicago, I alerted three employees
Who showed complete indifference towards me

United...
(United...)
You broke my Taylor Guitar
United...
(United...)
Some big help you are

You broke it, you should fix it
You're liable, just admit it
I should've flown with someone else
Orgone by car

'Cause United breaks guitars

When we landed in Nebraska,
I confirmed what I'd suspected
My Taylor'd been the victim
of a vicious act of malice at O'Hare

So began a year-long saga, of
'Pass the buck', 'Don't ask me',
and 'I'm sorry, sir, your claim can go nowhere'
So to all the airline's people,
from New York to New Deli
Including kind Ms. Irlweg,
who says the final word from them is 'no'

I heard all your excuses
And I've chased your wild gooses
And this attitude of yours, I say, must go

United...
(United...)
You broke my Taylor Guitar
United...
(United...)
Some big help you are

You broke it, you should fix it
You're liable, just admit it
I should've flown with someone else
Orgone by car 'Cause United breaks guitars

Well, I won't say that I'll never fly with you again
'Cause, maybe, to save the world, I probably would
But that won't likely happen
And if it did, I wouldn't bring my luggage
'Cause you'd just go and break it
Into a thousand pieces
Just like you broke my heart

When United breaks guitars

United...
(United...)
You broke my Taylor Guitar
United...
(United...)
Some big help you are

You broke it, you should fix it
You're liable, just admit it
I should've flown with someone else
Orgone by car

'Cause United breaks guitars

Yeah, United breaks guitars

Yeah, United breaks guitars

Source: https://www.musixmatch.com/lyrics/Dave-Carroll/United-Breaks-Guitars

EMPLOYEES AS HACKTIVISTS

It is a dangerous proposition but true as seen in many cases. An employee is a partner in building brands as they are frontal in customer engagement and service; therefore, it becomes paramount for employees to be the real brand ambassadors for any company. Brands such as Adobe, GE and Coca-Cola have structured employee brand ambassador programmes running in their companies. Employees to represent the company in front of its stakeholders is very important to a brand.

First, they are a more authentic source of information than a company-sponsored advertisement.

Second, when an employee starts promoting their company or brand on their social media handles, they draw a better emotional connect and purpose to the whole brand-building exercise of a company. Posts like 'how proud I am to work in XYZ company or for a brand' and what they are doing to add value to the consumers' lives and society at large are examples that are well perceived by stakeholders and keep the company or brand in good stead.

Finally, a company that encourages its employees to be the brand ambassadors builds pride in them and make them feel like a partner in the whole brand-building exercise. They are more committed and stay longer with the company.

But sometimes certain sections of employees could by mistake or deliberately damage the reputation of a brand by misadventure in the online space.

VIDEO PRANK THAT DAMAGED DOMINO'S REPUTATION

In 2009, two of the Domino's employees in America filmed a video prank contaminating Domino's food in the restaurant's kitchen by putting cheese up their nose and nasal mucus on the pizza and posted it online.[18] This was a bizarre food and health standard codes violation and, within a few days, the video got 1 million views on

[18] https://www.nytimes.com/2009/04/16/business/media/16dominos.html

YouTube and the company was in a deep PR crisis due to consumer backlash. Although they were fired and faced felony charges for delivering prohibited foods, the nightmare was not over for Domino's, as even customers who had a long run with the pizza giant were having a second thought of ordering pizza from them. The social media was flooded with negative comments about the brand and Domino's came out with a Twitter account @dpzinfo to manage all these negative comments which were hurting the brand image on social media. Even they came out with a video containing the CEO message that all was well, but all was not well and the damage was done.

If Gordon Ramsay saw this, he'd go from chef to serial killer in a split second.

👍 351 👎 REPLY

▾ View 4 replies

Thats why you should cook your own food at home!!

👍 126 👎 REPLY

▾ View 4 replies

Honestly animals are better than those dirty employees that are messing around with our food.

👍 64 👎 REPLY

▾ View 2 replies

The Internet is a double-edged sword. If it allows marketers to reach out to its consumers, it also has created new channels for consumers to communicate back with the brand. However, what goes online stays online. Customers refer to online reviews and brand action to develop perception and purchase intent towards a brand. Customers not satisfied with brands, unhappy employees and mistakes a brand does in the online space can all damage the reputation of a brand.

Troll Proof Branding in the Age of Doppelgangers

CEO CAN ALSO DO THE DAMAGE

Well, sometimes the CEO of a company who is the leader and the apex individual in an organization to build and protect its brands can also go wrong. This happened with one internal email forwarded by the CEO of UrbanClap, an Indian gig marketplace which offers home installation, maintenance and repair services, and home beauty and wellness services, to his employees that they should completely ignore a customer complaint, which then went on Twitter and Reddit and created damage to the reputation of the brand and the CEO.[19] Although the CEO later gave an arrogant one-sided explanation on this, but it did not help much.

REASONS FOR THE BACKLASH

> *Your most unhappy customers are your greatest source of learning.*
>
> Bill Gates (Microsoft)

There could be different motivations and intentions of consumers to hit back at a particular brand in question or brand avoidance.[20] Some reasons could be as follows.

1. **The gap between brand promise and brand delivery:** Consumers buy brands based on the brand promise communicated by the company regarding the brand performance. The moment there is a conflict between customer expectation and brand promise or brand promise and brand performance, the immediate result is that the customer reaches out to the company to resolve the issue, and if the

---

[19] https://inshorts.com/en/news/urbanclap-ceo-ccs-user-in-mail-asking-staff-to-ignore-him-1526452942371

[20] Lee, Motion & Conroy 2009.

customer service of the particular company is not trained enough, the customers are likely to express their anguish, discontent and anger on social media. From there it may go anywhere and may hit the brand in terms of reputation loss, customer loss or financial loss, or all of these.

2. **Brand authenticity gap:** Every brand has a unique way of positioning itself in the minds of the customer. The problem arises when the brand tries to portray a certain image of a brand, but the consumer does not perceive it that way.

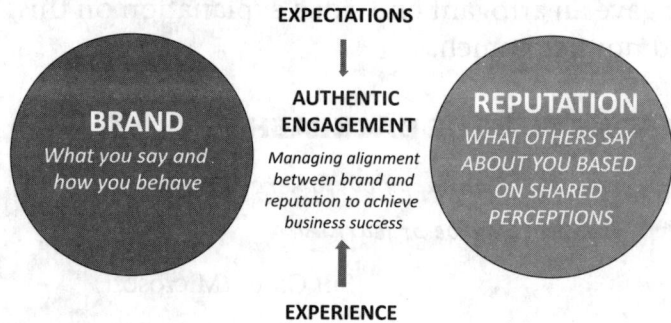

Source: FleishmanHillard.[21]

Cohn & Wolfe's 2017 Authentic Brands study ranked top 100 brands country-wise, based on the role of authenticity in business, the attributes associated with an authentic brand, and the impact of authenticity on the consumer, investor and employee attitudes and behaviours.

Top 10 Global Authentic Brands	Top 10 Indian Authentic Brands
1. Amazon.com	1. Google
2. Apple	2. Microsoft
3. Microsoft	3. Amazon
4. Google	4. Maruti Suzuki
5. PayPal	5. Apple
6. Addldas	6. Sony
7. Intel	7. YouTube
8. LEGO	8. BMW
9. BMW	9. Mercedes
10. HP	10. British Airways

https://www.youtube.com/watch?v=OhBmWxQpedI

3. **Moral avoidance:** This arises when a consumer feels that the brand's country of origin is a question mark. For example, Indians feel that products from China need to be boycotted due to them being responsible for Indo-China border tension or COVID-19 spread.[22] They show their discontent on social media to portray Chinese products and the country in a bad light. #boycottchina and #boycottchineseproducts have been doing the rounds on Twitter, and global users are participating and tweeting their reactions against the China misadventures.

KENNETH COLE #CAIRO TWEET

In 2011, Egypt was under turmoil as the Egyptians were protesting against the nearly 30-year reign of President Hosni Mubarak on its government's corruption. Kenneth Cole, an American fashion house, took this as an opportunity to use #Cairo to promote their spring line of clothing on Twitter.

> Millions are in uproar in #Cairo. Rumor is they heard our new spring collection is now available online at http://bit.ly/KCairo -KC
>
> 2 hours ago via Twitter for BlackBerry® ☆ Favorite ↄ Retweet ↱ Reply

People did not like the way brands like Kenneth Cole have used a serious issue as an opportunity for brand promotion. They made fake Twitter accounts and mocked the brand by tweets like these: 'Our new slingback pumps would make Anne Frank come out of hiding! #KennethColeTweets.'

[22] https://www.indiatvnews.com/business/news-boycott-chinese-products-india-china-lac-standoff-ladakh-cait-boycott-china-626880

Kenneth Cole's Response

Kenneth Cole realized their mistake and removed the tweet and issued an apology by the chairman on their social media handle, which read

> I apologize to everyone who was offended by my insensitive tweet about the situation in Egypt. I've dedicated my life to raising awareness about serious social issues, and in hindsight, my attempt at humor regarding a nation liberating themselves against oppression was poorly timed and inappropriate. Kenneth Cole, Chairman, and Chief Creative Officer.[23]

The question is: Are these little steps good enough to revive a brand image?

Well, hacktivism in the form of cyberattacks or that of individuals and groups on social media is a big threat for any brand. Brands have been devising counterstrategies where some are successful and some are not, as each company, corporate culture or situation is unique. But the companies have to prepare and have a strategy in place to protect their data and listen to the social media sentiments to take timely and appropriate action to respond to hacktivism against their brand.

---

[23] https://www.cbsnews.com/news/oops-kenneth-cole-apologizes-for-egypt-tweet/

CHAPTER 8

MEASURING BRAND DOPPELGANGER IMAGERY

If you don't give the market the story to talk about, they'll define your brand's story for you.

David Brier

A brand is a network of associations in the mind of the consumer, and they comprise of positive as well as negative brand associations. The paramount objective of a brand is to create and reinforce positive brand associations through brand elements (logo, symbol, jingle, colour, etc.), packaging and marketing mix (product, price, distribution channel and promotion). For example, Apple brand's associations are innovation, high technology, status, quality, expensive and stylish. Apple is all about a brand which is beyond commerce or products. It's about imagination, design and technology, and Apple consumers are loyal to the brand because they are emotionally connected with whatever apple does or creates. Apple is all about people more than products and has developed products around people. This helps it develop the Apple community, which supports and stands for the hopes, dreams and aspirations the Apple brand fulfils. When Nike was embroiled in the sweatshop controversy, it was not that consumers did not like their products, but it was that Nike had let them down and they went ahead culture jamming Nike's communication and creating a brand doppelganger of the brand Nike. So whether it is Nike or Tiger Woods, they all have to manage their negative associations in the mind of consumers, because if left to their own devices, these negative associations may create a monstrous brand doppelganger image and can destroy the brand equity.

According to Keller, brand image is defined as 'perceptions about a brand as reflected by the brand associations held in consumer memory'. Creating strong and unique brand associations is the top priority for any strong brand, and it helps brands to create positive perception towards themselves and gives reasons to consumers for purchasing or using a specific brand. When a consumer has an intent to purchase the process, they organize and retrieve information in their memory and use it logically and emotionally in favour of the brand which comes top of mind. Although positive brand associations help the consumer to develop an intent to purchase, the negative associations lead them to avoid the brand. So it is a matter of understanding that to be a preferred brand, a brand needs to have more strong and unique positive brand associations over the negative associations. Further, the brand needs to watch out that any negative brand association is not strong enough to overpower the cumulative strength of the positive associations. If we refer to the latest Ronaldo–Coca-Cola issue, the power of the negative brand association of being an 'unhealthy drink' created by footballer Cristiano Ronaldo by putting aside two bottles of Coca-Cola—the sponsor of EURO 2020—and recommending water instead has inflicted a $4 billion damage to the brand. So we see a new kind of 'sportsperson activism' in creating a brand doppelganger imagery of Coca-Cola as an 'unhealthy drink'.

In the past also, Coca-Cola brand has been attacked and has faced consumer backlash through fake news like 'Coca-Cola as a toilet cleaner' or trolled for 'peddling sugar', which has damaged the brand's reputation and value. So can brands like Coca-Cola ignore the creation of their doppelganger imagery or identify and measure its impact to develop a sound brand strategy? Brand health analysis is the most important predictive factor of company growth, and if you do not measure the strength and uniqueness of the brand associations and also the favourability of these brand associations, then you don't know how the brand doppelganger is getting created and how to counter it. Even strong brands need to be careful in managing the performance of their brand by continuously reviewing the performance of the brand. Marketing managers cannot accept even a slight slide in the brand value or overlook a single negative review about the brand. A brand's performance needs to be measured by monitoring certain key performance metrics to gain timely, accurate and actionable insights into brand health so that tactical and strategic decisions can be taken in the short and long terms. Well, positive brand associations will affect the brand equity positively, whereas negative brand associations will have a damaging effect on the equity of the brand.

HOW DOPPELGANGER BRAND IMAGES INFLUENCE THE MARKET CREATION PROCESS

Whenever there is an introduction of a new technology or medicine, there is a resistance to change, and their harmful effects in terms of expert opinions, experiments or fake news can get circulated in the popular culture, creating a new kind of brand image—the doppelganger. According to Markus Giesler, a consumer sociologist and marketing professor at the Schulich School of Business at York University, 'It may be through a progressive sequence of contestations between the brand images promoted by the innovator and doppelganger brand images promoted by other stakeholders that concrete exchange structures between producers and consumers are established and a market is created.' The COVID-19 pandemic and the success of market creation of the vaccination process are dependent on the buying of the vaccine benefits by all the stakeholders, whether for or against the vaccination drive. Many experts have come forward and shared their thoughts on mass vaccination and how it can have side effects too. One such expert has been Nobel Laureate and prominent French virologist Luc Montagnier, who quoted that mass vaccination can lead to mutation of the coronavirus. Post his comments, there was a tsunami of fake news taking rounds on social media platforms claiming that the Nobel Laureate has said that people who are vaccinated will die after two years.[1] This could create a strong doppelganger for the vaccination drive in India and influence negatively the market creation for the India-manufactured vaccines such as Covishield and Covaxin. The Indian government and PIB Fact Check had tweeted that the news circulated was fake and, therefore, had tried to do damage control and urged the public not to circulate the news.

---

[1] https://www.indiatoday.in/fact-check/story/fact-check-nobel-laureate-luc-montagnier-didn-t-say-covid-vaccine-recipients-will-die-in-two-years-1807023-2021-05-26

Giesler, who researched the brand doppelganger imagery of Botox Cosmetic treatment, the number 1 cosmetic treatment for frown lines, crow's feet and forehead lines, concluded that there is a contradiction between the technology claim and what some actors in the stakeholder network perceive. The gap is the doppelganger brand imagery of Botox Cosmetics. He used the 'actor–network theory' from sociology to measure the impact of the Botox doppelganger on the market creation process of the self-enhancing technology. The argument is that the new technology may contradict the natural process and hence will have negative connotations or associations around its usage and effects. For example, vaccines for immunity boosting will always be up against the natural process of developing immunity or a protein supplement for a gym-goer will always lose an argument against natural protein from poultry, dairy or seafood. The main benefit of protein is that it contains amino acid which breaks down in the body and helps build your muscles. Dairy-based protein supplements like whey protein obviously will provide the required amino acid, but it has preservatives and added colour, which may harm the body. So it is always recommended to take protein from natural sources. Self-enhancing technologies like Botox rely on emotional branding, which has led to its doppelganger brand imagery comprising of 'poison', 'frozen face', 'Frankenstein' and 'junkie'.

The hermeneutic analysis as conducted by Giesler on the Botox brand imagery clearly shows that for each of Botox's emotional brand story, there is a brand doppelganger imagery reaction.

Botox Emotional Branding Story   **Botox Doppelganger Imagery**

Fun & happiness	Contradictions	Botox kills you
Health & vitality	Contradictions	Freezes your expression
Love & compassion	Contradictions	Makes you a zombie
Time & efficiency	Contradictions	Is addictive
Freedom & Independence	Contradictions	Fun & happiness

Source: M. Giesler, 'How Doppelgänger Brand Images Influence the Market Creation Process: Longitudinal Insights from the Rise of Botox Cosmetic', *Journal of Marketing* 76, no. 6 (2012), 55–68.

Botox Cosmetics has been promoting its technology as a wellness therapy and has been compared by its consumers with yoga/spa/painting as it enhances the self and lives up to its tagline 'For Me, Myself and I'. Although the emotional consumer connects drew many towards the brand, it also led to the cultural backlash with stories around the product ingredient botulinum toxin type A taking rounds as a poisonous substance used for biological warfare by Islamic terrorists. So the 'actor–network theory' can help identify the various brand doppelganger imagery created by the stake-holders and help marketers to develop a strategy to cir-culate brand stories to counter the negative imagery

Troll Proof Branding in the Age of Doppelgangers

created particularly in the course of the diffusion of an innovation.

SENTIMENTS DO MATTER

No matter whether a brand is good or bad, or right or wrong, people will talk about it. A stronger brand is more vulnerable to the brand doppelganger. People like to talk about those who are successful and express their sentiments through online mediums, particularly social media microblogging sites. So if a customer is happy with a brand, they may share their experience on social media and when unhappy would like to pull the brand down by posting negative sentiments. Since people have become more expressive on social media regarding sharing their sentiments for a particular brand experience, it is therefore essential for brands to understand the sentiments of their stakeholders online. Sentiment analysis is a process of finding out the positive or negative sentiments about your brand and is useful to address those sentiments which may harm the brand. In 2013, before Diwali, the festival of light in India, PepsiCo ran a Twitter contest inviting people to tweet their version of Ramayana with #Ramayana140. This led to social media backlash against the brand, and PepsiCo had to withdraw the promotion stating that the objective was to involve the young Indians to participate in India's most celebrated festival but it backfired.

...

Sita probably loved another man before she met Ram. #ramayana140

♡ 2   ⟲   ♡ 2   ⬆

...

We apologize that our #Ramayana140 contest has unintentionally caused some concern to consumers. Our intent (cont) tl.gd/n_1rqsjj4

♡ 109   ⟲ 117   ♡ 15   ⬆

Customer opinion, feedback and reviews are very important, and sentiment analysis can help you analyse whether your customers are happy about your marketing mixes such as product quality, delivery and performance or they are decoding your promotional mix the way you have designed it to be decoded. Sentiment analysis models focus on a certain methodology based on polarity that if people are positive or negative towards the brand, it may help the marketer discover the consumer's purchase intention towards the brand or whether the consumers are happy, disappointed or annoyed with the brand performance or promise. The brand polarity sentiment analysis can use the five-point scale to gauge the level of positive sentiments people may have towards the brand.

Sentiments Polarity - five point scale

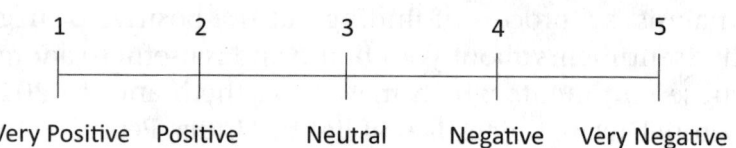

IPL Sentiment Analysis July 2021

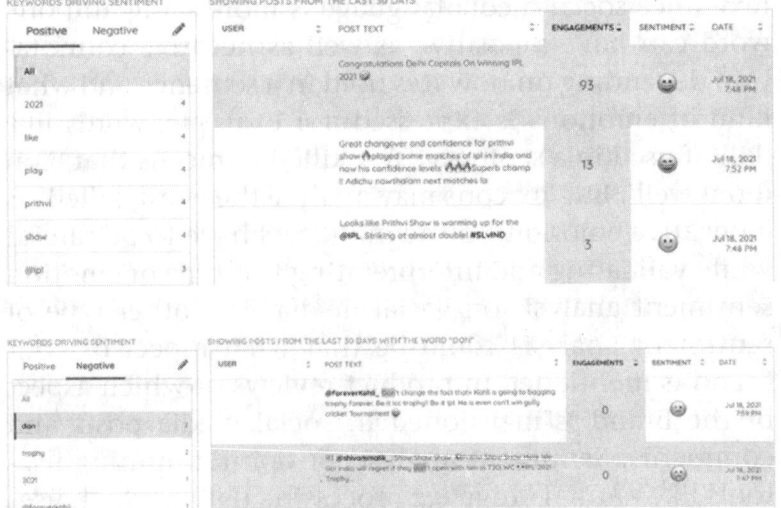

Source: https://Keyhole.co

Twitter sentiment analysis of IPL for the period 4 July 2021–18 July 2021 shows that around 68 per cent of tweets were neutral (the one in blue), around 24 per cent positive and only 8 per cent negative. Probably since IPL is not played during this period, the tweets are more neutral than positive or negative, which means that people are not expressing strong opinions about the sporting event. Marketers besides polarity would also like to analyse the emotions displayed by social media users towards the brand. They want to analyse that if the customer is happy, sad, disappointed, frustrated, annoyed and angry with the brand, they would like to address the negative emotions and reinforce the positive ones. Lexicons, all the words which are used in a subject or particular language and the emotions they convey, are used by many social media emotion detection platforms and tools. Some may use complex machine learning algorithms to detect emotions in the text posted about the brand by social media users. A lexicon is a good method of detecting emotions in the text since social media language is more slang and one word can have a positive as well as negative connotation depending on how it is used in a sentence and what kind of emotions is expressed; for example, words like 'kill' if used in a sentence 'You killed it' means that 'You did it well'. But lexicons may analyse the word 'killed' as a negative emotion, so the marketers have to be careful while validating and interpretating this type of emotion sentiment analysis on social media. The other type of sentiment analysis could be that what aspect of your brand is mentioned in product reviews or which aspect of the brand is mentioned in social media posts and comments. Sentiment analysis or opinion mining uses tools like natural language processing (NLP), which uses machines to analyse human speech with NLP or through machine learning algorithms. Sentiment analysis algorithms could be based on manually crafted rules or machine learning techniques could be used to gather, analyse and interpret data. The importance of sentiment analysis cannot be undermined as it helps businesses to track the sentiment of their customers towards their brand. Businesses through machine learning techniques can sort the sentiment posted on social media in the form of conversations, reviews, posts, comments, etc. This helps businesses to get deeper insights into consumer behaviour and analyse the impact of their brand communication for better decision-making. Every day, data is created online by UGC through blog posts, tweets, surveys, reviews and articles, so managing this big data manually is impossible and therefore sentiment analysis helps to sort this data for sound business decision-making, particularly to develop a strategic digital marketing plan. Since the data is in real time, it helps businesses to restrict the amplification of any negative sentiment in no time, saving it from the creation of brand doppelganger.

LEARN TO LISTEN, LISTEN TO LEARN

To understand what the consumer is feeling about the brand, the brand needs to listen to the conversations on social media as to what the customer is posting, commenting and tagging and the hashtags used by them to mention their brand. They need to listen and understand what issues are raised by their customers and how to solve these issues through social listening. Social listening involves analysing the social media conversations and trends about a brand, brand category and industry as a whole. So it is not a matter only when someone mentions or tags a brand, but the brand needs to have a deeper understanding of why, where and how these conversations are generated to gather insights for better brand-building strategies. There is a difference between social media monitoring and social media listening, where monitoring refers to monitoring social media's direct messages concerning a brand and responding to them.

Airtel, India's largest telecommunication service provider, has recently made a promise to its customers to monitor and resolve their complaints in a mission to deliver best-in-class services to customers. The whole idea behind the campaign is to bring the customer complaints to 'zero' by resolving them in no time. For this, they are using their Twitter handle @airtel_presence (Airtel Cares). According to Shashwat Sharma, Chief Marketing Officer, Bharti Airtel,

> The relationship between Airtel and its customers has never been more important, and to serve them even better we have decided to take our customer obsession to the next level. We know that 'ZERO questions' is an IMPOSSIBLE utopian thought especially for a telecom brand, but that won't stop us from trying because we know that the closer we get to ZERO, the happier our customers will be. We promise to be humble, learn every time we fail

183

and be relentless in our approach. For us, this is not just a campaign, we are now re-engineering the entire organization towards this goal and are obsessed with building a culture of consumer centricity.[2]

Airtel Cares ✓
@Airtel_Presence

The Official 24/7 customer support handle for @airtelindia. Hearing from you help us to serve you better :) DM us for quick resolution.

⊙ India   🔗 airtel.in   📅 Joined January 2010

On the other hand, social media listening helps to understand the conversation threads around your brand or industry or any topics relevant to your brand and develop a strategy to address the same. For example, a brand needs to listen to the social media conversations even if it is tagged or mentioned. For example, a brand like KFC will gather insights into people's perception about fried chicken and why they are mentioning it without mentioning KFC.

So if someone posts 10 delicious recipes of fried chicken, KFC will be keen to know how it is different from those and what is it that people prefer as ingredients so that they can develop variants around the people choice of fried chicken. Also, if people are cooking fried chicken at home, KFC would like to understand the recipe, process, occasion, etc.

A social listening strategy though seems difficult, but machine learning algorithm makes it easier to analyse the brand mentions and anything around your brand and industry which may be relevant for the brand. Suppose you run a fast-food restaurant and want to understand the food your customer prefers. So you can use social media listening tools to understand and analyse customer conversations by creating product themes.

[2] https://www.airtel.in/press-release/06-2020/airtel-promises-to-go-the-extra-mile-for-its-customers

Performance		Conversations		Demography		Themes		Message		
Themes										
Theme	Volume	Share of Voice (%)	Engagements	Likes	Comments	Shares	Potential impressions	Positive Mentions	Negative Mentions	
Burgers	870	7.2	12,709	8,756	2,178	623	1,737,895	826	89	
Wraps	247	3.4	7,727	3,412	1,986	49	456,677	240	54	
Fries	222	2.9	545	298	980	10	227,310	111	21	
Nuggets	114	1.8	1,078	879	132	13	197,771	95	7	
Pizza	112	1.2	87	78	88	18	44,955	102	9	
Happy Meal	95	0.72	346	123	198	13	36,324	52	20	
Coffee	52	0.52	4,958	1,897	1,341	9	115,146	23	8	

The above representative data gives you insights into your offerings.

- Burgers have the maximum positive and negative mentions. So the brand needs to listen to what these positive and negative comments are and develop strategies around them.

- Happy Meals do not have many mentions but has a maximum percentage of negative comments. So the brand needs to revisit its strategy and resolve customer pain points which are culminating in negative comments.

- Pizza is not discussed very frequently but has a high number of positive mentions. So the restaurant needs to promote pizza more.

SOCIAL MEDIA LISTENING LEADS TO A HEALTHY BRAND

Understanding customer sentiments through social media listening will give insights into the positive and negative conversations associated with your brand or product offers. You can get answers to a lot of questions about the brand's health, for example:

- What are people talking about my brand or product and how long is the conversation thread?

- Is the brand perception moving in a positive or negative direction?

- What are people talking about my brand? What aspect of my brand is of concern or pain point for people?

- How strong is the brand doppelganger image, means how damaging are the negative associations created in social media conversations?

SO WHAT SHOULD A BRAND DO?

- Create answers for all the frequent questions or doubts the customers are expressing in their comments by creating an FAQ.

- Respond to issues raised by customers in no time.

- Work on your strengths as that is why customers love you.

- Create a social media response team and chatbot to resolve the issues and initiate a dialogue with your customer.

Social media listening is not only limited to text mining to understand whether the sentiments are positive or negative and then convert them into standardized or aggregate data metrics. But innovation in machine learning can now analyse natural language, videos and photos, helping digital marketers to analyse sentiments expressed in text or pictorial or video form to make sound business decisions. Companies like Starbucks have strong visual imagery so they capture the image mentions through image recognition technologies because if they don't do that, then they may miss out on the customer who is using Starbucks coffee cups to start a conversation, whether positive or negative. Well, a picture is worth a thousand words (text)!

- Tylenol, the pharma brand for headaches and migraines, learned through its social media listening of the messaging boards and forums of the knitting community that due to long hours of knitting, people develop migraines. So Tylenol adjusted its social media strategy to reach out to the knitting community which led to an increase in the web traffic on the Tylenol website.

- Netflix on the other hand invented Netflix Socks after listening that many people go to sleep while binge watching. It introduced Netflix Socks which detect when the user is sleeping and pauses the programme. This got Netflix to win the Shorty Award for creative use of technology. According to Netflix, 'When we aren't posting, we're listening, looking for the new trends igniting the entertainment world.'

- L'Oréal uses social media listening to fuel its product development strategy. They identify industry and consumer trends and keep an eye on ratings, reviews and conversations around the L'Oréal brand and products. According to the company's market insight and data manager, 'Social allows us to refocus our actions on the present moment, tracking and adapting in real-time to continuously improve the link with our consumers.' So, when L'Oréal was confused about which hair colour it should launch from ombre, tie-dye or splat, it researched the UGC on YouTube and identified influencers from a set of thought leaders and analysed Google trends to develop its new hair colour L'Oréal Feria Wild Ombre.

- Taco Bell, one of the most innovative social media companies, uses comedians and GIFs to interact with their customers. They use social media listening for customer care and create campaigns and develop new products. According to Taco Bell, 'Instead of sitting behind glass and listening to a focus group, we now have access to 20 million consumers and can be inspired by them and connect with them and have real relationships with them.' Well, they are right, as surveys and focus groups have their limitations of small sample size and biased results which become outdated in no time. Taco Bell not only engages with its customers on social media by retweeting positive mentions but also deals with customer complaints, particularly when a set of customers were not happy with the cheese in Quesalupa. The company immediately informed the stores as to how to follow the Quesalupa recipe for customer satisfaction.

CASE STUDY
Virgin Holidays Trending Travel Guide: Created through Social Media Listening

Virgin Group, a British multinational founded by Richard Branson and Nik Powell in February 1970, has been known for its marketing maestro. Their airline venture has been in news for innovative marketing strategies and changing the way we travel. Fighting the status quo and championing customer experience has been the core mantra of the Virgin brand. Virgin has been aggressive in its above-the-line and below-the-line marketing initiatives. Digitally, through its marketing agency ForwardPMX, Virgin has been active in its digital marketing strategy by using digital components for search engine optimization, content marketing, paid and organic search, social media strategies and data analytics.

Though the brand was performing well during the peak holiday or travel times through aggressive advertising but was low on performance in Google ranking, particularly their brand 'Virgin Holidays'. The holiday travel space is mapped by all of its competitors and off-season brand performance took a hit. In order to navigate the peak and off-peak travel performance, Virgin Holidays discussed its concern with its agency ForwardPMX to develop a digital strategy for the off-peak season. This discussion transpired into creation of Virgin's 'Trending Travel Guide', one of its kind travel guide, using social media listening technologies and data analytics tools to create engaging content to increase brand awareness and image building.

The travel target audience is becoming younger and is very active on social media for their travel information and planning. They do Google search for their travel requirements and are generally exposed to keyword-led articles on travel and that too of low-quality content on the search engine result pages. Virgin jumped to this opportunity and used social listening to capture the real-time consumer conversations related to travel from their social media post, comments, etc.

ALL EARS TO SOCIAL MEDIA

The Virgin's Travel Holiday team analysed the social media posts and studied the positive and negative sentiments reflected in the post regarding the travel destinations and ranked holiday attractions which can be recommendations for those who are making their holiday plans. The Trending Virgin Holidays guide created a real-time traveller's guide in competition or alternate to review sites like Tripadvisor. The whole idea is to collate authentic recommendation through user experience in real time. This gives the brand an opportunity to engage with consumers throughout the year and create engaging content based on the consumer insights and recommendations.

The Trending Travel Guide

Welcome to the Virgin Holidays' Trending Travel Guide — featuring the latest posts, top tweets and inspirational imagery from the most iconic holiday hotspots around. Get ready to set some new holiday goals.

New York | Las Vegas | Orlando | Caribbean Islands | Barbados

Source: https://trending.virginholidays.co.uk/

The Virgin Trending Travel Guide website reads, 'We've got recommendations from millions of social media posts, bringing everything you need for vacation inspiration under one roof. Let social media (and us) be your travel guide'. The guide analysed over 28,372,998 social media posts for New York including Facebook, Twitter, etc., to find the top-mentioned attractions, restaurants and shopping places that were posted on the social media handles of the consumers. For example, the top-ranked attractions in New York included Times Square, China Town and Central Park. New York restaurants featuring at the top spots as per the social media mentions were Peter Luger Steak House, the Modern and Eataly NYC Flatiron and the top shopping mentions included Barneys, NYC Garment District and Groupe NYC.

Virgin used social listening application programming interface integration through Crimson Hexagon, integrates social data measurements into web services and mobile applications to perform big data analysis across multiple systems. The data analyses resulted in listing the most popular restaurants, bars, nightclubs, attractions, museums, waterparks, casinos and more across Virgin Holidays US destinations. The data was updated automatically every day to give the current popularity of these destinations in real time.

DIGITAL PR OUTREACH

Virgin PR carried out the link-building exercise through the Virgin PR outreach programme including articles in the business marketing magazines, design websites, travel news websites and travel writer partnerships and tied up with travel influencers to create engaging content and attract traffic to their site driving conversions. Virgin used its paid and organic search team and customer relationship management teams to promote their 'Trending

Travel Guide'. They also leveraged their partners like bloggers to promote it on their social media handles and websites.

Cana L Street, Chinatown, Nyc   •••

unicorn as your dinner date 🦄
185 w

185 w   1 like   Reply

185 w   1 like   Reply
——— View replies (1)

185 w   1 like   Reply

933 likes
MAY 24, 2018

Log in to like or comment.

Source: https://www.instagram.com/p/BjJOZfbgl24/

OUTCOME

- The Virgin 'Trending Travel Guide' witnessed a 286 per cent increase in traffics through back links from 287 referring domains.

- The Virgin 'Trending Travel Guide' was ranked among the Top 10 travel sites.

- The site traffic included 8,500 new users.

- Total page views recorded were 20,000.

- The click through rate increased by 75 per cent to the landing page.

- The Facebook impressions recorded were 812,000.

According to the media and digital spokesperson of Virgin Holidays, 'Most travel brands voice their

Troll Proof Branding in the Age of Doppelgangers

respective opinions on where to go and why, but we felt there was an opportunity to try a different approach. We knew conversations about travel experiences were happening at scale and that there is heavy reinforcement of recommendation through social proof. We wanted to find an innovative way to tap into these conversations and present them back to our customers. Essentially, we felt that the power of thousands of individual experiences and suggestions aggregated together could be a hugely beneficial reinforcement'. The Virgin Travel Guide changed the way the content is created for the travellers with a new school of thought away from the conventional travel aggregator sites such as Trivago and Tripadvisor. These conventional sites were found to be publishing fake reviews created by the hotels and destinations. In some cases, people were paid to write positive or negative reviews. So breaking the norm, Virgin Travel Guide created a platform which only published content and recommendations from real-time consumer social media posts on travel and tourism. Virgin used the power of social listening to analyse millions of social posts to bring the users trending attractions and locations around the globe.[3]

MEASURING BRAND DOPPELGANGER IMAGERY

Consumers generally develop brand associations, whether positive or negative, in their minds from their brand exposure or/and experience. This brand experience can be a collective interaction with the brand messages through various mediums or first-hand experience with the brand.

---

[3] https://www.thedrum.com/news/2019/01/11/virginholidays-launches-the-trending-travel-guide-with-forward3d
https://trending.virginholidays.co.uk/
https://www.forwardpmx.com/case-study/virgin-holidays-trendingtravel-guide/

Consumers Internet 2.0 world is not a passive audience to the brand messages; they believe in two-way communication with the brands. They are not shy of expressing their support or discontent towards a particular brand. These consumers then express their attitude towards the brand by posting their expressions on social media platforms (Facebook, LinkedIn, Twitter, YouTube, etc). These cultural backlashes create the monstrous doppelganger brand imagery—the negative consumer-generated stories circulated on the Internet through social media. The central questions about these brand backlash and social criticisms are: Do they hurt a brand and should a company take action to combat them? This viral culture-jamming phenomenon influences the brand associations in the consumer minds. Brands which follow emotional branding strategies create an opportunity for the emergence of a doppelganger brand image, and big brands are more vulnerable to the doppelganger brand imagery phenomenon. Researching, analysing and managing this monstrous phenomenon is of paramount importance to brand marketers. Marketers need to identify and analyse the substantive insights into people's emotions, metaphors, non-verbal communication, and text and visual expressions of their displayed sentiments in evaluating the brand performance or influencing brand associations. So despite analysing the consumer sentiments online and offline, it is essential to understand their thoughts and behaviour which leads to an emotional outburst against the brand story.

BRAND CONCEPT MAPPING

Brand doppelganger imagery can be measured by analysing positive and negative brand associations which require a scientific procedure, validity and reliability of the research methods applied. Marketers need to understand the substantive knowledge of the thoughts and behaviour of their consumers. They need to bring out the consumers' deeper feelings, thoughts and behaviour towards their brand and understand the premise of these consumer insights. Most of the thoughts are image-based and not word-based as two-thirds of all stimuli reach the brain through visual sensory. Therefore, most of the brand communication has to be visual. Also, most of the communication which marketers need to understand is non-verbal. They need to not only rely on quantitative approaches of collecting and analysing consumer insights but also apply qualitative techniques to capture the non-verbal cues and process them systematically to develop mental maps for better understanding of their consumers. Also, marketers should understand the use of metaphors in consumer communication, as metaphors are central to thought and imagination. Consumers may use metaphors to express their experience or perception towards a brand, and metaphors are important to elicit hidden knowledge towards a brand. Mark Johnson from Chicago University once said, 'Without imagination, nothing in the world, could be meaningful. Without imagination, we could never make sense of our experience. Without imagination, we could never reason towards knowledge of reality.' Metaphors help the medical fraternity to understand their patients' unconscious experiences in more conscious communication to understand their mental state. Metaphors are important because if you see it from consumers point, it hides the thoughts, but the metaphor conveys their meanings and consumers' expression towards the brand if analysed properly. So don't ignore the metaphors! Traditional research methods like focus groups are not able to find meanings to these metaphors which are important to uncover the mental construct of the consumers.

Furthermost thoughts, emotions and learnings, as mentioned by Gerald Zaltman, Professor Emeritus at Harvard Business School, occur without awareness. Feelings are just the tip of the iceberg; it is the conscious emotional state or reaction, and most emotions are cognitive functions guiding the consumers' thoughts and behaviour without awareness. Consumers' developmental maps are based on their sensory experience with the brand. These brand constructs are developed by organizing brand associations and connecting them to the brand and each other to create a

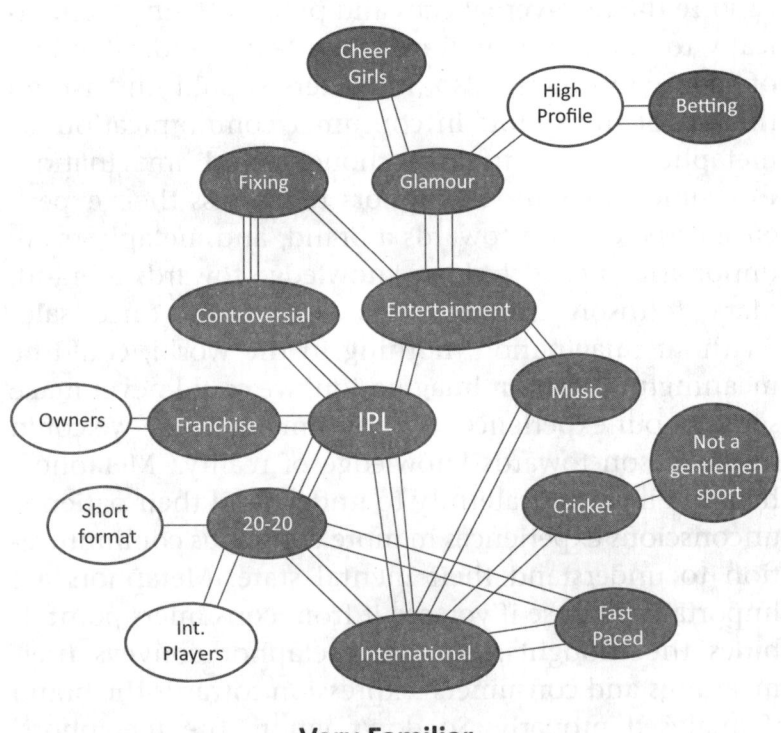

Very Familiar

Source: G. Sood and J. K. Sharma, 'An Empirical Research into IPL's Brand Doppelganger Using the Brand Concept Mapping Technique', *International Journal of Public Sector Performance Management* (2021). doi:10.1504/IJPSPM.2021.10039726

Troll Proof Branding in the Age of Doppelgangers

brand mental map. So marketers need to identify relevant constructs and brand associations' positions in these constructs. Brand associations are associations which come to the consumers' minds when they think about the brand. There are different methods for eliciting brand associations from consumers. Some of these methods are free association, attribute rating scales and brand concept maps. In free association, a typical response to the question 'What comes to your mind when you think of Apple?' may include brand image attributes/benefits (e.g., technology and IOS operating system), its products (e.g., iPhone, iPod and MacBook Air) and people (e.g., Steve Jobs).

But very few of these methods can elicit (getting information/reactions from people) the network of these associations in the consumers' minds. So a network of an association like in the IPL example will have a first-order association which is directly linked to the brand and second-order associations which are indirectly linked to the brand. Most of the techniques cannot distinguish between the first- and second-order associations except the brand concept mapping (BCM) technique. Also, the BCM technique is the recommended methodology for analysing the impact of brand doppelganger on the brand imagery.

The application of brand concept maps, which elicits first- and higher-order brand associations which do not need skilled interviewers can be administered on a large sample of respondents belonging to different demographics and psychographic segments. The application of the BCM technique produces individual consumer mental maps from positive and negative brand associations and then produces an aggregated map—an aggregation of the individual maps. Brand concept maps can answer the following questions for the marketers to analyse the strong, unique and favourable brand associations and also the weak, non-favourable and negative brand associations.

- Which are the positive or negative brand associations?
- Which are strong (linked directly to the brand) or weak (linked indirectly to the brand) brand associations?
- How can marketers build strong, unique and favourable brand associations?
- Would any change in the brand associations result in the change of brand network and impact the imagery of the brand positively or negatively?

CREATING BRAND CONCEPT MAPS

According to John, BCM, a methodology for identifying brand association networks, comprises of three stages:[4]

1. **Elicitation stage:** Wherein the brand associations are elicited from the consumers

2. **Mapping stage:** Wherein consumers map the elicitation to show how they are connected to the brand and each other

3. **Consensus mapping:** Wherein the researcher develops a consensus brand map from the individual brand maps and associated data

Zaltman's metaphor elicitation technique (ZMET): Zaltman and Coulter[5] have described step by

[4] D. R. John, B. Loken, K. Kim, and A. B. Monga, 'Brand Concept Maps: A Methodology for Identifying Brand Association Networks', *Journal of Marketing Research* 43, no. 4 (2006): 549–563.

[5] R. H. Coulter and G. Zaltman, *Using the Zaltman Metaphor Elicitation Technique to Understand Brand Images* (ACR North American Advances, 1994).

step these three stages in detail to understand consumers' thoughts about brands. The elicitation stage involves a small number of respondents (30–40) who use photographs and images followed by an in-depth personal interview to elicit construct. The interviews use qualitative techniques to capture verbal constructs such as Kelly's repertory grid and laddering exercises. This is followed by the mapping stage where the researcher reviews the individual constructs and asks the respondent to develop a map which shows the important connections among important constructs. The researcher then develops a consensus map in the aggregation stage in which the researcher reviews the important constructs and maps from the respondent's data to develop a consensus map which shows the important connections among important constructs. The researcher after reviewing decides on which constructor's construct relationships are important to be included in the consensus map. The researcher here makes sure that he/she includes the most frequently mentioned constructs and develops a connection between the constructs to develop a consensus map.

Although ZMET has its advantage, as it is a thorough technique to elicit brand associations, it also employs various qualitative techniques to capture verbal and non-verbal consumers' expressions. It ZMET establishes reliability and validity with the brand, but validity between the associations is still an issue with the ZMET method. Despite ZMET being labour-intensive and needing expert researchers, it has limited flexibility in constructing brand maps from the elicitation, mapping and aggregation stage, as they are so intertwined.

Brand concept map on the other hand is a technique where consumers are asked to elicit brand associations and map them linking each associated with the brand or with other associations and create a network of association. Then these individual associations are scientifically analysed and a BCM measure is constructed for the associations elicited from the consumers. An example of brand concept map measure for IPL fans is given below.

BCM Measures for IPL Fans							
	Core Associations			First-Order Associations			
A	B	C	D	E	F = E/C × 100	G = C − E	H = D − G
S. No.	Brand associations	Frequency of mention	Number of interconnections	Frequency of first-order mentions	Ratio of first-order mentions (%)	Subordinate connections	Superordinate connections
1	Cricket	108	128	64	59.3	44	84
2	Entertainment	97	106	41	42.3	56	50
3	20-20	89	101	75	84.3	14	87
4	Franchise	89	97	68	76.4	21	76
5	Music	85	69	39	45.9	46	23
6	High paced	83	93	55	66.3	28	65
7	International	83	126	46	55.4	37	89
8	Fixing	82	103	42	51.2	40	63
9	Glamour	81	85	37	45.7	44	41
10	Controversial	77	108	59	76.6	18	90
11	Not a gentleman's sports	77	94	32	41.6	45	49
12	Cheer girls	77	66	27	35.1	50	16
13	Short format	74	99	34	45.9	40	59
14	High profile	74	51	24	32.4	50	1
15	Betting	68	84	27	39.7	41	43
16	Star owners	65	74	18	27.7	47	27
17	International players	62	42	33	53.2	29	13
18	Black money	47	54	33	70.2	14	40

BCM Measures for IPL Fans

A	Core Associations			First-Order Associations	$F = E/C \times 100$	$G = C - E$	$H = D - G$
S. No.	Brand associations	Frequency of mention	Number of Interconnections	Frequency of first-order mentions	Ratio of first-order mentions (%)	Subordinate connections	Superordinate connections
19	Sponsors	45	25	21	46.7	24	1
20	Parties	42	33	25	59.5	17	16
21	Contests	22	29	11	50.0	11	18
22	Conflict of interest	11	13	2	18.2	9	4
23	Players' conflict	7	12	4	57.1	3	9
24	Overdose of cricket	4	7	2	50.0	2	5
25	BCCI	4	3	2	50.0	2	1

Source: G. Sood and J. K. Sharma, 'An Empirical Research into IPL's Brand Doppelganger Using the Brand Concept Mapping Technique', *International Journal of Public Sector Performance Management* (2021). doi:10.1504/IJPSPM.2021.10039726

After applying the brand concept map method and capturing the brand associations through consumers' perception about IPL and plotting them in a network of associations, reliability and validity of the analysis can be conducted to check the quality of research by checking the consistency and accuracy of the measures applied. Although the brand value of IPL has increased over the years, the negative sentiments attached to match-fixing, etc., still haunt the sporting league. Despite monstrous negative imagery created by the stakeholders in the past, the brand has overcome its doppelganger as it has changed its nature and form by adopting a more entertainment format away from a gentlemen sport. Although the negative brand associations of IPL created a lot of controversy and discussions in all quarters of stakeholders, fans, authorities, experts and media, it did not affect the purchase intentions in terms of crowds in stadium or viewership and sponsorships. Well, they say that even negative publicity is publicity!

Brand concept maps' contribution towards the measurement of the brand doppelganger image cannot be ignored. It not only identifies the network of brand associations and how strongly, uniquely and favourably they are connected to the brand but also helps marketers analyse the impact of each association in the network and how any change in the strength of one association can have an impact on the brand image. Marketers practise different branding strategies to create an emotional story around the brand with positive associations, but they are at risk too. Marketers need to be tracking the alternate brand stories circulated by their stakeholders in the popular culture and listen to consumers and analyse the culture backlash creating the brand doppelganger. They should address the issues raised by the disgruntled customers and give them solutions by developing a strong customer relationship management system. Marketers should also test their brand stories and how stakeholders are decoding them; for example, a brand may have a very good product but poor after-sales service, a gap between brand promise and brand performance. Lastly, all the internal stakeholders should be aligned and trained to handle any such creation of brand doppelganger and raise an alarm before the doppelganger imagery becomes monstrous.

CHAPTER 9

COUNTERSTRATEGIES

Your brand is the single most important
investment you can make in your business.

Steve Forbes

The Web is a dangerous place with people trying to sabotage the brand equity through culture jamming, trolling, fake news, digital activism and opposing the brand's emotional branding stories, creating a brand doppelganger, a family of critical and uncomplimentary stories circulated in the popular culture by anti-brand activist, social media users and opinion leaders. These disparaging images, if ignored, can lead to the creation of brand doppelganger and can damage the brand's reputation and can question its authenticity by negatively affecting the brand equity. Brands try to build a positive network of brand associations in the mind of consumers by fostering a strong emotional connection between the brand and the consumers. A brand image which is the perception about the brand in the mind of consumers acts as a brand differentiator and builds powerful brand equity, but big brands are more vulnerable to the brand doppelganger. From memes to parodies, adbusters and subvertising, a brand doppelganger can originate from anywhere and in any form. It can be created by consumers, anti-brand activists, competitors, opinion leaders, media and the public at large, who help in amplifying the brand doppelganger image by circulating it through their social media platforms.

BRAND SCORING THEIR OWN GOAL

Not all brand doppelganger is created by outsiders; sometimes, the company scores its own goal by committing itself to a strategic blunder by mistake. In 1923, Joseph Dequeker started a small chocolate factory known as 'Italo Suisse' and later on moved its base from Izegem, a municipality located in West Flanders, Belgium, to the city Roeselare, Belgium, in the 1930s. In 2013, the brand underwent a rebranding exercise and named it 'ISIS' to get away from its Italian roots towards Belgium origin.[1] But after the upsurge of the terrorist outfit Islamic State of Iraq and Syria (ISIS), the brand got a bad name, as people started relating it to the terrorist group. According to the company's director Ignace Libeert, the ISIS name backlash had had a significant impact on the brand and created negative associations of the brand which led to a loss of 2–3 million euros. Although this whole episode was not in control of the company, it happened without knowing what the future stores for the brand. So if the company retains the name 'ISIS', they should be prepared for brand avoidance and further financial loss. But the brand decided to rebrand it with a new name from 'ISIS Chocolates' to 'Libeert'[2] to disassociate itself from the Islamic militant group.

---

[1] https://www.scmp.com/news/world/article/1625188/belgian-chocolate-company-decides-isis-not-good-trading-name

[2] www.libeert.com

LISTEN AND RESPOND TO YOUR CUSTOMERS

Sometimes listening to your customers can resolve a lot of customer frustrations. Brands chose to overlook customers complaints arising from the gap between brand promise and brand performance. These customer's relationship with the brand is fragile and even if it is strong, the customers get disappointed when their favourite brands do not listen to their complaints and take no action to resolve them. When the customer loses hope and gets no response from the company, they let their frustration out by telling the whole world through their social media pages to make the brand realize that each customer is important and it is the customer who buys their product and services which makes them a great brand. So the customer may resort to culture jamming by way of parodies, memes and satires of the brand and their experience with the brand creating a brand doppelganger. Award-winning Dave Carroll's guitar got damaged by the freight handlers of United Airlines on which he was traveling. So after no response from the airline, Dave decided to do a satire on the airline through his song 'United Breaks Guitars' and dented the brand reputation of the airline, creating a brand doppelganger. United Airlines learned its lesson after the consumer backlash and improved and trained their customer relationship management and started responding to each customer query or complaint. Not only this, they also developed a new customer escalation policy and strengthened their social media strategy to respond to such negative brand mentions and started managing the negative social media sentiments thereon.

LOYAL CUSTOMERS WILL FIGHT FOR YOU

Loyal customers are the backbone of any brand. According to a smartphone loyalty report from Sellcell.com,

America's number one phone trade-in site, Apple mobile phones' brand loyalty has reached an all-time high staying at 92 per cent up from 2019 from 90.5 per cent.[3] This is way ahead of its competitor Samsung's brand loyalty by 18 per cent. Brand loyalty comes into question when a customer decides to upgrade their product, and 26 per cent of Samsung users generally tend to move to other brands while upgrading their devices. Apple devices have all been named with the prefix 'i', and it is the signature prefix for the Apple products such as iMac, iPhone and iPod. Although the presumption is that the 'i' is the individual customer or user of the Apple devices and that Apple is a customer-centric brand and will always innovate products that focus on increasing the productivity of its customers, but literally, as could be understood from Steve Jobs in 1998 at the launch of iMac, 'iMac comes from the marriage of the excitement of the Internet with the simplicity of Macintosh. We are targeting this for the number one use that consumers tell us they want a computer for, which is to get on the Internet—simply and fast.'[4] So the 'i' stands for the Internet.

Apple's innovation iPod changed the way music was consumed, and this followed with products such as iPod Shuffle, iPod Nano and iPod 5th Generation. This innovation of Apple made the competing MP3 player companies like SanDisk worried and ran a campaign 'iDon't' to create a brand doppelganger of the Apple iPod brand. The campaign used animals listening to music on the iPod, including zombies, sheep, donkeys, chimps, cows, puppets, etc. They used phrases such as 'iFollow', 'iSheep', 'iHerd', 'the walking iDead', 'have you become

---

[3] https://www.sellcell.com/blog/cell-phone-brand-loyalty-2021/

[4] https://appleinsider.com/articles/18/05/06/20-years-ago-the-imac-changed-the-world

an iPuppet?' and 'are you an iChimp?' The idea behind this was to demean the Apple iPhone and question the users not to develop a herd mentality and move towards iPods but think and buy SanDisk's Sansa e200, a portable media player. Although Apple was slow to respond, Apple's loyal customers took SanDisk 'iDon't' campaign on social media. Also, sometimes it is better not to respond to such malicious intent of your competition and let the public decide. So SanDisk campaign failed not only as people rejected its negative campaign against iPod but also because its products failed to compete on features such as memory, price and battery life as compared to iPod.

MANAGING BRAND DOPPELGANGER

Brand doppelganger comes in many forms and through anonymous sources; therefore, it is difficult to manage the impact of the monstrous doppelganger. Marketers need to develop a strategy to combat the brand doppelganger imagery, and they have to research the following:

- What form has the brand doppelganger adopted to destroy the brand's reputation? Is the brand culture jammed through memes, anti-brand websites, blogs, satire, parody, fake news, trolls, digital hacking, etc.?

- Is the brand doppelganger positive and favours your brand as in the case of the IPL or is it damaging or is it accidentally created by company's mistake or market social, political, economic or cultural environmental changes?

- How will the brand doppelganger damage the brand? Will it result in reputation loss, financial loss, brand avoidance, etc.? Also, how strong is the brand doppelganger, and what is the extent of damage it may cause?

- What are the options available to combat the monstrous imagery?

DO NOT IGNORE THE NEGATIVE BRAND ASSOCIATIONS

The bigger the brand, the more vulnerable it is to the brand doppelganger imagery. The paramount objective of the brand is to develop strong positive brand associations in the minds of its customers. Nike's Swoosh, Apple's 'i' prefix products, Nokia's ringtone or Titan's signature tune, Kellogg's Tony the Tiger, film stars with Lux soap and so on are the few examples of brand associations that have a classic impression in the minds of consumers over a long period across generations. Brand image is the perception about a brand reflected in terms of brand associations that are seeded in the minds of its customers. Therefore, brand associations are connected to the brand directly or indirectly, and the network of brand association represents the meaning the brand holds in the mind of the customers. Brand associations play an important role in developing and implementing brand strategies and in the consumer's decision-making journey. Brand strategies are developed to create strong, unique and favourable brand associations to differentiate the brand from its competitors to position the brand in the minds of customers, in brand extension, to create brand equity, and give reasons to consumers to buy and consume the brand. Consumers on the other side develop the network of brand association in their minds to process and organize brand information and use it when making a purchase decision. So when you think of a brand, certain associations come to your mind. These could be positive or negative based on the customers' experience or perception. A brand image is very fragile, and any mistake can ruin its reputation and lead to brand avoidance. The brand has to quickly get into damage control and regain customer confidence; otherwise, it may lead to the creation of brand doppelganger and customer loss.

Johnson & Johnson pain relievers over-the-counter (OTC) brand Tylenol faced negative brand associations when in 1982 people got killed after consuming Tylenol extra strength capsules. Later, it was discovered that these killer capsules were laced with poisonous potassium cyanide by someone with murderous intentions.[5]

After this negative imagery, Tylenol suffered a loss in market share from 35 per cent to 8 per cent. So Tylenol recalled the 31 million bottles in circulation, offered to replace the capsules that people would return and also announced a reward for providing them with the information as to who is behind poisoning the OTC brand. After spending $100 million, Tylenol was able to manage this PR crisis and was able to reverse the negative association due to the incident and changed the way we buy and consume OTC medication. Tylenol team worked with the US Food and Drug Administration (FDA) to make a new tamper-proof packaging with foil seals which became the industry packaging standard for OTC medicines.

The world obesity ranking puts the USA at number 12 with 36.2 per cent, and much of it is credited to the junk food served by fast-food restaurants like McDonald's and other food joints.[6] McDonald's has always been criticized for its high-fat content food and its 'super-size' or large portions like 200 g of French fries and 1.25 l glass of Coca-Cola. In 2004, Morgan Spurlock

[5] https://www.nytimes.com/2002/03/23/your-money/IHT-tylenol-made-a-hero-of-johnson-johnson-the-recall-that-started.html

[6] https://obesity.procon.org/global-obesity-levels/

directed a documentary featuring him eating at the McDonald's all of his meals for one month. When he ordered food at McDonald's, the restaurant employee pushed the option of converting his standard meal to 'super-size'. The result was that he added 25 pounds to his body mass, and the doctor advised him to stop eating the junk food as it might damage his liver. This became a nightmare for McDonald's UK, as sales dropped and the company removed the super-size portions from its menu and added healthier options such as salads and milk and launched its new campaign 'Every Step Matters'. They promoted the benefit of exercise and gave away pedometers.

Samsung's Galaxy Note 7, the 5.7 inch phone with a stylus, got negative associations attached to its smartphones due to its Lithium-ion battery explosion while on charging, which caused the phone to catch fire that even burnt a user's house. The negative association was so strong that it brought the sale of the smartphone giant down by 15 per cent. It was bad news for the company, as its competitors such as Apple and Google were launching their new phones in the market. Samsung recalled, refunded and replaced all the Note 7 smartphones and found out after a lot of testing and research that the Note 7 battery was bigger to fit in the case and therefore it expanded and exploded when heated during charging. To get the trust of its consumers back, Samsung accepted their mistake and explained the root cause of the battery explosion, and communicated it to its stakeholders. It did change the internal culture of the company from a cold-hearted company to a warm, consumer-centric company. Samsung acknowledged its accountability in the Note 7 fiasco and worked towards a new purpose for the company's smartphone division. Pio Schunker, the senior vice-president of the mobile phone division at Samsung, said, 'We became a cultural meme, a daily announcement on every flight and there was wave after wave of negative commentary—not just from the press, but from consumers as well.'[7] He, further quoting the fiasco, said,

> We knew we couldn't afford the luxury of a fetal position and just lie there, so the first thing that we did to make things right was to take accountability. For Samsung, it wasn't just the right thing to do, it was the only thing to do.[8]

The new purpose that Samsung discovered so that it could become the most preferred smartphone brand and that the stakeholders could rally around it was a new tagline which was targeted to the employee and the customers: 'Do What You Can't'. The Samsung revenue went up by 95 even at the time of this crisis.

CASE STUDY: H&M'S COOLEST MONKEY IN THE JUNGLE ADVERTISING CAMPAIGN

H&M, a Swedish fashion retailer with a net sale of SEK187 billion in 2020, has around 4,913 stores in 74 global and 53 online markets. It globally has 120 million members in its loyalty programme and 71 per cent women employees in responsible positions in the company. In January 2018, H&M faced a strong consumer backlash for its ad featuring Liam Mango, a five-year-old Kenyan black model, wearing an H&M hoodie sweatshirt which read 'Coolest Monkey in the Jungle'.[9]

---

[7] https://www.businessinsider.in/tech/from-a-cultural-meme-to-a-comeback-kid-how-samsung-overcame-its-galaxy-note-7-fiasco/articleshow/60970681.cms

[8] Ibid.

[9] https://www.pagecentertraining.psu.edu/public-relations-ethics/introduction-to-diversity-and-public-relations/lesson-2-how-to-reach-diverse-stakeholders/reaching-diverse-stakeholders-externally/

H&M was accused of racist slurs against the black community for comparing them with a monkey.

H&M soon realized their mistake among growing consumer backlash on social media and removed the advertisement from their online store. Later, the company issued an apology posted on the company's website stating,

> We agree with all the criticism that this has generated—we have got this wrong and we agree that, even if unintentional, passive or casual racism needs to be eradicated wherever it exists. We appreciate the support of those who have seen that our product and promotion were not intended to offend but, as a global brand, we have a responsibility to be aware of and attuned to all racial and cultural sensitivities—and we have not lived up to this responsibility this time.[10]

But probably this was not enough for those criticizing the brand, so H&M took various other corrective measures and initiatives to win the consumer trust back in the brand. Some of them are as follows:

- Appointed a Black American to head their inclusion and diversity division
- Twelve people will screen the advertisement before it is uploaded
- At least five people will do the quality check at each stage of the advertising creation process
- Will ensure diversity in leadership and, by 2025, H&M will be a 100 per cent equal opportunity company

Result

H&M not only faced consumer backlash but also financial loss with over $4.3 billion in unsold clothing,

----

[10] https://about.hm.com/zh_cn/news/general-news-2018/h-m-issues-unequivocal-apology-for-poorly-judged-product-and-ima.html

and the share price dropped on the ground that H&M lacked diversity. 'We also acknowledge our past mistakes and they have made us acutely aware of how much we still need to learn. As a company, we are growing, but we can and must do better,' stated Helena Helmersson, CEO of H&M Group, 'We recommit to taking tangible steps to challenge racism and support our colleagues, customers, and communities. Symbolic support is not enough—we will take action.'

LESSON LEARNED: GET YOUR APOLOGY RIGHT THE FIRST TIME!
Control the Narrative; Don't Let the Narrative Control You

In 2017, 'fake news' became the 'Word of the Year' in *Collins English Dictionary* and since then, it has become a powerful tool to spread misinformation and rumours to destroy a brand image and create a brand doppelganger. A brand needs to give a strong, clear and timely response to the fake news because it may be in the nick of time that the misinformation about your brand goes viral. So it is important for the brand to be the first to learn about the fake news in circulation and for that, it needs to constantly monitor news and activate social media listening to map the chatter around the brand. Before major damage is done to the reputation of the brand, it needs to launch a communication campaign with its stakeholders, including the source of the fake news to replace the fake information with facts. The brand needs to check the transparency of its communication and processes to the stakeholders and provide them with easy processes to verify and clear any doubts created with the circulation of the fake news. The brand has to adopt a data-driven strategy with an empathetic and more human approach. All of us have gone through the interactive voice response (IVR) system of any brand's customer service management. It takes too many options to get the response you desire or speak to the customer service executive. Isn't it frustrating? Yes, it is, as the automation, processes and data should be used more empathetically, taking into account the shifting needs of consumers with a soft-scaling approach.

The brand needs to develop strategies keeping in view the changing social–economic, political and technological changes in consumer behaviour. Hero MotoCorp Limited, formerly Hero Honda, an Indian multinational motorcycle and scooter manufacturer headquartered in New Delhi, India, launched its new programme 'Just4her' for female customers who were uncomfortable or intimidated to visit the Hero Honda showrooms and buy the two-wheeler. The company responded to the changing demographic shift in two-wheeler buying and launched women-exclusive showrooms driven by all-women staff and designed like a boutique studio rather than a two-wheeler traditional showroom. The brand-target audience always wants the brand to understand their changing needs and provide solutions for a smooth brand–customer relationship. If fake news is circulated about the brand, the brand needs to replace it with the facts and prove the fake news wrong with an authentic communication strategy. Customer testimonials can rescue the brand, as they are not the company's employees and will always come out with the real brand experience to counter the fake news. Identify the source of fake news and come out with a timely counterstrategy to control the amplification of the fake news across all customer touchpoints or channels. Brands should remember the 'Streisand effect' and its consequences, so it has to be very careful if engaging with the fake news. Sometimes, it is important to address the issue without bringing it up in the public eye. Lastly, a brand should sensitize its employees and prepare them to counteract the effects of fake news and protect the brand image.

Travis Trammell, a predoctoral fellow of the Program on Democracy and the Internet (2019–2020) at Stanford University, USA, has developed an offensive model to counter the fake news.

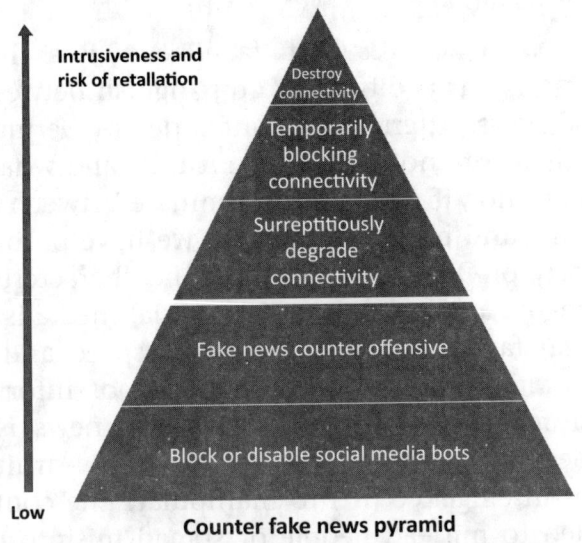

Source: T. I. Trammell III, *Fake News Risk: Modeling Management Decisions to Combat Disinformation* (Stanford University, 2020).

According to dictionary.com, 'Bots, a software program that can execute commands, reply to messages, or perform routine tasks, as online searches, either automatically or with minimal human intervention.' Bots help companies answer customer queries, and some may use it for spreading misinformation and fake news on social media. Bots on social media are automated accounts which look managed by real people but are used to spread fake news. One study suggests that 9–15 per cent of Twitter accounts are bots and the firm Ghost Data suggests that around 95 million bots are posing as real accounts on Instagram.[11] Facebook data shows that

[11] https://indianexpress.com/article/technology/tech-news-technology/about-9-15-of-twitter-accounts-are-bots-study-4566555/

they had disabled 6.5 billion bots in the year 2019. Although all these efforts have come to post the damage done to many brands, more such efforts are welcome to reduce the speed of these bots used to amplify the fake news propaganda.

Barak Obama believes that 'fake news' is a threat to democracy, as it is difficult to distinguish between fake and real news. Attending a conference in Germany, he stated, 'If we are not serious about facts and what's true and what's not, if we can't discriminate between serious arguments and propaganda, then we have problems.'[12] The worry of Obama is right, but the characteristics of social media are contrary to this. Social media is a platform that favours gossips, creativity, speed and shareability or amplification of the spread of information or misinformation. The threat of fake news is more from 'deepfake', which leverages machine learning and artificial intelligence (AI) to manipulate the content of the video to mislead people or spread misinformation through these fake but real-looking videos. Even the Facebook CEO and founder Mark Zuckerberg was not spared by deepfake, and a fake video was released on Instagram showing him talking about world domination. According to the CEO of Hero Collective, a social media marketing company based out of New York,

> The rise of deep fakes on social media is a series of cascading issues that will have real consequences around our concept of freedom of speech. It's extremely dangerous to manipulate the truth when important decisions weigh in the balance, and the stakes are high across the board. Viral deepfake videos don't just damage the credibility of influential people like politicians, brands, and celebrities;

---

[12] https://www.theguardian.com/media/2016/nov/17/barack-obama-fake-news-facebook-social-media

they could potentially cause harm to our society by affecting stock prices or global policy efforts. Though some people are creating them for good fun and humor, experimenting with this technology is like awakening a sleeping giant. It goes beyond goofing off, into the manipulative and malicious territory.[13]

So how do you stop or reduce the impact of fake news? Well, it is a story of AI vs AI. so for every deepfake, there is deep learning. Therefore, to stop the amplification of fake news, AI and machine learning have developed an automated detection system known as deep learning techniques used to detect fake news from real news. However, fake news is not easy to detect, as it not only requires detecting the fake news and comparing it with the real news but also eliminating the subjectiveness and bringing in a more scientific method of comparing the two. Another technique to detect fake news is 'stance detection', which detects the relationship between the two texts in the news, for example, the relationship between the headline and the body copy, and tries to find if any relationship between the two exists or not. Whether the body copy and headlines can be similar or not will depend on the stance between them in terms of 'agree', 'disagree', 'discuss' or 'unrelated'. So as a matter of strategy, the idea is to slow down the amplification of the fake news by slowing the master bot.

According to Facebook, most fake news is financially motivated to gain economic incentives. The more the news is amplified, the more the financial gains for the promoters of fake news. Facebook is working to fight the spread of fake news by

- 'disrupting economic incentives because most false news is financially motivated;

---

[13] https://www.forbes.com/sites/tomtaulli/2019/06/15/deepfake-what-you-need-to-know/

- building new products to curb the spread of false news; and

- helping people make more informed decisions when they encounter false news.'

Brands can also launch a counteroffensive on the prompter of the fake news by questioning the credibility of the originator and exposing their real intentions to the public. Besides brands, even the governments are worried about the damage fake news is causing in their countries. One of the Indian states in India, West Bengal, is considering a legislation to jail people who are spreading misinformation which may cause fear or alarm in the public.[14] The Indian government has issued guidelines by making provisions in the Indian Penal Code (IPC) and the Information Technology Act (IT Act) through Section 505(1) of the IPC 1860, which states, 'Whoever makes or circulates a false alarm or warning as to disaster or its severity or magnitude, leading to panic shall be punished with the imprisonment which may extend to one year or with fine.' The black hole of fake news WhatsApp has been alleged for being the delivery vehicle for fake news which has incited many violent incidents in India. India has many times shut the Internet services to stop or slow down the spread of fake news through WhatsApp. This is done by the complete blackout of the Internet services or slowing it down on mobile phones. Under pressure from the new Indian IT law, WhatsApp blocked two million accounts between May 2021 and June 2021.[15] Ninety-five per cent of these users were blocked for surpassing the forwarding limit of a

[14] https://economictimes.indiatimes.com/news/politics-and-nation/west-bengal-plans-new-law-to-tackle-fake-news-on-social-media/articleshow/64598026.cms?from=mdr

[15] https://www.thehindubusinessline.com/info-tech/whatsapp-bans-2-million-accounts-under-new-it-rules/article35346248.ece

WhatsApp message. The misinformation spread during the COVID-19 pandemic break has even led the Director-General of the World Health Organization to quote, 'We are not just fighting an epidemic; we are fighting an infodemic. Fake news spreads faster and more easily than this virus, and is just as dangerous.'[16]

DON'T FEED THE TROLLS

Trolls will demonstrate aggressive behaviour while engaging with you on social media. They will engage in meaningless arguments, be sarcastic on various social, political and economic issues, and will do anything to seek attention. No matter how much you are politically correct, trolls will break into your defence, no matter what. So whatever your business is or who you are, trolls make sure that they need to culture jam the brand and create negative doppelganger imagery. The more followers, connections or friends you have on social media, the more vulnerable you are to trolling. Not all trolls are anonymous or invisible; many of them will have a real account and may have a popular social media presence and could also be a dissatisfied customer. Brands need to spot the trolls through social monitoring and have to strategically respond or decide not to respond based on their marketing disposition.

TROLL THEM RIGHT BACK

Although a brand needs to be cautious when they want to take the troll head on, it may open the Pandora's box of more toxic conversations. The rule of the game is to ignore the troll and not to feel it. But to save your brand reputation and counter the troll, a brand needs to troll the troll.

[16] https://www.who.int/director-general/speeches/detail/munich-security-conference

The only thing the brand needs to be concerned about is to make sure that the troll is not your dissatisfied customer as the approach should change then. Troll back like Wendy's! Wendy's, an American international fast-food restaurant chain, has been playing the clever troll game with its competitors and customers for a long time and in most cases has been winning the troll game. Wendy's has locked horns with its competitors, both McDonald's and Burger King, on Twitter. Wendy's decided to troll McDonald's claim of 'Our beef is flash-frozen to seal in fresh flavor' and compared it with the iceberg that sank the Titanic in its Super Bowl advertisement and promoted the freshness of its own 'never frozen beef'. Wendy's continued to roast McDonald's on Twitter and cleverly trolled the troll no matter if it is the competitor itself, McDonald's, or any die-hard fan of McDonald's.

Similarly, when it's other competitor Burger King trolled the brand in 2016 by introducing a counteroffer to Wendy's '4 for $4 meal' by its offer of '5 for $4' and claiming it to be a better offer, Wendy's immediately trolled back.

DON'T FUEL THE TROLL, IGNORE THEM

Trolls are attention seekers. They want to get under your skin and irritate you with all kinds of critical and derogatory comments on social media. Well, the best response is to ignore them, but if you are a bigger brand, it may be a tricky situation. They say if you ignore the troll, you fail to fuel them, and hence they will go away. Experts believe that engaging with trolls is like extending their life, and a brand may lose its narrative while fuelling the troll. Also, social media attention spans are short and any troll can have a life not more than few days and will die its death with the new trending thing on social media. Brands' paramount objective is to serve its customers, and if the trolls are not giving any financial blow to the brand, it should ignore. Brands need not react to every troll but should respond to genuine concerns of its customers or instances where there is a huge social media backlash and public sentiments at large are going against the brand story like in the case of Tanishq, wherein the jewellery brand had to discontinue its advertisement involving interfaith couple after strong social media backlash. Sometimes brands find it difficult to ignore and land up into controversy. Swiggy, a food-delivery app, got its foot in the mouth by getting sandwiched between Twitter users from different political spectra. Swiggy responded to Finance Minister Nirmala Sitharaman's parody account tweet mentioning 'Bhakt', a right-wing activist. Swiggy got mixed trolling from those who supported it for calling 'Bhakts' as uneducated, and others trolled with derogatory comments and called for #boycottswiggy.

> Had an argument with my Bhakt friend over farmers protest.
>
> He said that we are not dependent on farmers for food. We can always order food from Swiggy.
>
> He won.
>
> 432   1.9K   16.5K
>
> **Swiggy** ✔ @swiggy_in · Nov 30, 2020   ...
> sorry, we can't refund education 🎓
>
> 2.2K   9.3K   35.9K

BE DISCREET WHILE YOU TROLL

Not always your brand is trolled by your dissatisfied customer, anti-brand activists or bot, but you can also be trolled by another brand. Just be careful the way you respond or troll back to this friend of yours. Keep it on the lighter side with witty trolling and make sure that you are not offensive or rude in your social media engagement with another brand. After all, you all are in the business with one objective: to serve the customers by maximizing profits. So treat the brand that is trolling you with due respect as you want the other brand to respect you. So when Amazon India took a jibe at the food delivery app Zomato for rebranding its logo almost six times in a short period. Zomato took it on its stride and trolled, mocking the Amazon A-Z logo and engaged in a fun thread with the e-commerce giant.

•••

.@Zomato Loved all the logos you used in the last 6 months. Was #AurDikhao the brief to your designer? :)

   ♡ 21   ⇅ 318   ♡ 255   ↑

Replies

•••

Replying to @amazonIN
.@amazonIN You should've seen the ones that didn't make the cut ;)

Replies

•••

Replying to @zomato
@Zomato That put a smile on our face ;)

So whether it's fake news promoters, trolls, hacktivists, culture jammers, anti-brand activists or any dissatisfied customer or competitor, the objective is to undermine or attack the perceived authenticity of a brand and create a 'doppelganger brand imagery'. Most of the brands have fallen or struggled against their doppelganger and have faced reputation or financial loss. It does not matter what branding strategy is developed by the marketers, it still is vulnerable to the creation of the brand doppel-ganger. Brands can build a mousetrap to trap customers or get a mindshare for their brand or devise emotional or cultural branding strategies to build its brand's authenticity, but still they are vulnerable to the attack on their brand reputation and creation of a brand doppelganger.

MONITOR CONSUMER TRENDS AND SENTIMENTS

The brand should be aware that its branding story is reaching its maturity stage or that its perceived brand authenticity has come under attack and is beginning to develop a doppelganger brand image. The brand needs to monitor the extent of this doppelganger image by empirically analysing the reach and impact of this imagery on the brand associations network by applying the BCM methodology. So the brand should be concerned as to what part or aspect of its branding story is under attack. For example, is its customer service, product features, benefits, price, distribution channel, etc.? And what alternative image or brand meanings are getting created?

COCA-COLA VS PEPSI

In the USA, Coca-Cola is an iconic brand and a cultural brand icon. But with Pepsi positioning itself as 'The Choice of New Generation', it outsold Coca-Cola, where consumers had a choice to decide which cola brand to buy particularly in retail outlets as compared to where they might not have a choice, for example, a McDonald's outlet. So by the 1980s, Coca-Cola's share started declining from 24.3 per cent in 1980 to 21.7 per cent in 1984. This worried the brand, as more households preferred to stack Pepsi and even the business tie-ups were a worry as Burger King decided to serve Pepsi to its consumers and not Coca-Cola. So Coca-Cola increased its promotional spend almost 33 per cent more than the Pepsi's promotional budget. With the new Pepsi positioning targeting the youth, suddenly Coca-Cola found itself on the older side and tried to fight the young image of Pepsi by offering discounts and increasing its promotional budget, but nothing helped!

So Coca-Cola did market research on focused groups to find out the reason for changing consumer preferences through a 'taste test' and discovered through the research results that it was the taste which was the major differentiator between the two cola giants. Pepsi got the King of Pop Michael Jackson to endorse the brand and Coca-Cola settled for Bill Cosby, the number one TV host, to promote the brand. Coca-Cola then did a taste test and developed a new formula different from (but close to) Pepsi's taste and away from the classic Coca-Cola. The new Coca-Cola with a new flavour passed the taste test against the original Coca-Cola and Pepsi. But soon after the new Coke launch, there was a widespread consumer backlash.

The loyal Coca-Cola consumers considered Coke as an American cultural icon and were disappointed and angry that Coke had discontinued the product. It took just 80 days for Coke to realize their mistake and relaunched the old Coke and named it 'Coke Classic'. Slowly, they faded the 'New Coke' from the market and continued with their iconic original Coke.

The Coca-Cola Company failed to read the associations the American consumers had with Coke and according to the Coca-Cola Company itself, 'The Coca-Cola Company took arguably the biggest risk in consumer goods history, announcing that it was changing the formula for the world's most popular soft drink, and spawning consumer angst the likes of which no business has ever seen.'[17]

The marketing blunder of Coca-Cola even has a mention on the Coca-Cola Company's website, as it has changed the dynamics of the cola market, and the rivalry between Coke and Pepsi continues with a neck-to-neck fight for the global market share.

Source: https://www.coca-colacompany.com

Brands should continuously monitor consumer sentiments across the Internet and look for any anti-brand discussions and should immediately strategically address the issue. Brands should assess when their branding story is transpiring into consumer cultural backlash and what form the cultural jamming has taken. The frequency and level of intensity of the cultural backlash need to be assessed and managed in a quick turnaround time.

---

[17] https://www.coca-colacompany.com/company/history/the-story-of-one-of-the-most-memorable-marketing-blunders-ever

MANAGE YOUR LAPSED OR DISSATISFIED CUSTOMERS

A brand needs to learn why its consumers are buying it, but more important is to understand the sentiments of those who are not buying or have shown interest but have not bought the product. A brand should be concerned about those who are lapsed or dissatisfied customers and are avoiding the brand due to the negative doppelganger image. It should use BCM techniques to assess which brand association is originated or influenced by the doppelganger image and derive the deeper meaning of these associations in the consumer's mind. Sometimes the brand doppelganger imagery is based on certain ideological differences as created and amplified by anti-brand activists, but it may have little or no influence on consumer brand avoidance. As it was clear from the IPL case that even though the doppelganger was strong and had developed many negative brand associations, still the brand did well because the controversies created had only helped the brand because the IPL DNA is not that of a 'gentleman's game' but is more towards 'entertainment'. Therefore, the brand associations like match-fixing, glamour and money helped in creating brand hype and curiosity among its stakeholders. Similarly, Starbucks's anti-brand activists created the brand's negative image around predatory business practices, whereas the consumers perceived that brand authenticity was around Starbucks lacking a personal touch.

STAY AHEAD OF THE CULTURAL CURVE

A doppelganger's brand image possesses many challenges, and to stay ahead of the cultural curve before your branding strategies, lose their steam and become a branding crisis. The moment a brand realizes that a brand doppelganger image might get created, it should launch a new branding strategy in alignment with the brand's marketing objectives. Any brand story, if continued for long, can result in diminishing returns on investment and the brand may struggle at the decline stage of its brand story and may suffer declining sales and profits. If a brand loses its cultural claim to authenticity, as we have seen in many examples in this book and in most of the cases, the brand is forced to withdraw or correct its branding strategy. The brand needs to revitalize its branding strategy and create a cultural ideology to establish an emotional connection with its target audience. Giesler[18] introduced a four-step brand revitalization process which could be adopted by the brand to stay ahead of the cultural curve.

FOUR-STEP BRAND IMAGE REVITALIZATION PROCESS

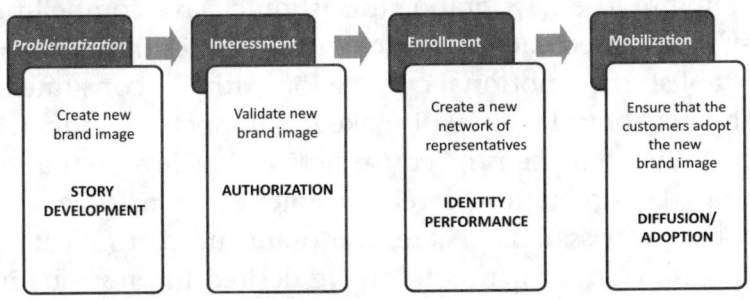

Source: M. Giesler, 'How Doppelganger Brand Images Influence the Market Creation Process: Longitudinal Insights from the Rise of Botox Cosmetic, *Journal of Marketing* 76, no. 6 (2012): 55–68.

[18] M. Giesler, 'How Doppelganger Brand Images Influence the Market Creation Process: Longitudinal Insights from the Rise of Botox Cosmetic, *Journal of Marketing* 76, no. 6 (2012): 55–68.

Problematization, defamiliarization of common sense, is the first step to identify the doppelganger image and analyse its elements which are creating a contradictory cultural ideology to the brand story. Based on the findings, marketers should develop a new brand story which is aligned with their marketing goals. For example, IPL, started in 2008, came up with its first advertisement build around the rivalry of the players and teams and was called 'Karamyudh'. Later, in the years 2012 and 2013, IPL was gripped by the controversies of spot-fixing[19] and betting, and in 2015, it changed the focus of its advertisements from cricket or players to 'India ka Tyohaar', creating a new brand story of festivity and entertainment away from the gentleman's game. After the creation of the new brand story, the brand must validate the claims made and how it resonates with the cultural ideology of the brand. Remember that the consumer is influenced by the doppelganger imagery and, therefore, the new brand story should have compelling research-based facts, data or customer testimonials to establish the emotional connection with the consumers. The new brand story will make the doppelganger image irrational, but then the consumers will believe in it after clear demonstration or endorsement by customers or brand ambassadors. There, the brand needs to create a new network of actors to create desired impressions in the consumer's mind. In the end, use IMC such as advertising, PR and digital marketing to circulate and amplify the new brand story.

A powerful doppelganger image may indicate that a brand has reached its maturity stage and can either allow it to decline or revitalize the brand by the creation of a

---

[19] https://www.firstpost.com/sports/ipl/ipl-spot-fixing-live-bookies-talked-about-fixing-3-more-players-787311.html

new brand story. Although in some cases (Congress party in 2014 general elections), it may have been too late to identify the emergence and impact of the brand doppelganger, paying the price by reducing it to 44 seats in the Indian parliamentary elections, in another case, it may act as a warning sign, and the brands reading the writing on the wall immediately create an extension to the brand story aligned with its cultural ideology and marketing goals (IPL, Nike, Starbucks, United Airlines and many more).

BIBLIOGRAPHY

Aaker, D. A. 'Managing Brand Equity: Capitalizing on the Value of a Brand Name'. *Journal of Marketing* 56, no. 2 (1992): 125–128.

Aaker, D. A. *Brand Relevance: Making Competitors Irrelevant.* Chichester: John Wiley & Sons, 2010.

Aaker, D. A. *Building Strong Brands.* New York, NY: Simon & Schuster, 2012.

Aaker, D. A., and R. Jacobson. 'The Financial Information Content of Perceived Quality'. *Journal of Marketing Research* 31, no. 2 (1994): 191–201.

Aaker, J., S. Fournier, and S. A. Brasel. 'When Good Brands Do Bad'. *Journal of Consumer Research* 31, no. 1 (2004): 1–16.

Abi-Ezzi, N. 'An Analysis of the Treatment of the Double in the Work of Robert Louis Stevenson, Wilkie Collins, and Daphne du Maurier'. Doctoral diss., University of London, 2000.

Aggarwal, P., and A. L. McGill. 'Is That Car Smiling at Me? Schema Congruity as a Basis for Evaluating Anthropomorphized Products'. *Journal of Consumer Research* 34, no. 4 (2007): 468–479.

Ajzen, I., and M. Fishbein. *Understanding Attitudes and Predicting Social Behaviour.* Englewood Cliffs, NJ: Prentice-Hall, 1980.

Arora, R., and C. Stoner. 'A Mixed Method Approach to Understanding Brand Personality'. *Journal of Product & Brand Management* 18, no. 4 (2009): 272–283.

Barhorst, J. B., and A. Wilson. 'Retweeting Brand Experiences: Factors Motivating Receivers to Proliferate Brand Image Disruptions'. Choosing the Right Tools for the Job. MMA Spring Conference Proceedings. Marketing Management Association, USA, 2017.

Barreda, A. A., A. Bilgihan, K. Nusair, and F. Okumus. 'Generating Brand Awareness in Online Social Networks. *Computers in Human Behavior* 50 (2015): 600–609.

Batey, M. *Brand Meaning: Meaning, Myth and Mystique in Today's Brands*. Oxfordshire: Routledge, 2015.

Belén del Río, A., R. Vazquez, and V. Iglesias. 'The Effects of Brand Associations on Consumer Response'. *Journal of Consumer Marketing* 18, no. 5 (2001): 410–425.

Berger, J. *Contagious: Why Things Catch On*. New York, NY: Simon & Schuster, 2016.

Berger, J., and K. L. Milkman. 'Emotion and Virality: What Makes Online Content Go Viral?' *GfK Marketing Intelligence Review* 5, no. 1 (2013): 18–23.

Berry, L. L. 'Cultivating Service Brand Equity'. *Journal of the Academy of Marketing Science* 28, no. 1 (2000): 128–137.

Bhattacharya, S., and S. Bhattacharya. 'Auction of Players in Indian Premier League: The Strategic Perspective'. *International Journal of Multidisciplinary Research* 2, no. 2 (2012): 16–36.

Biel, A. L. 'Converting Image into Equity'. In *Brand Equity & Advertising: Advertising's Role in Building Strong Brands*, edited by David Aaker and Alexander L. Biel, 67–82. East Sussex: Psychology Press, 1993.

Brandt, C., C. Pahud de Mortanges, C. Bluemelhuber, and A. Van Riel. 'Brand Concept Maps: A Method of Capturing Doppelgänger Brand Image'. 2010. Available at: http://hdl.handle.net/2268/137297

Brown, S. 'Where the Wild Brands Are: Some Thoughts on Anthropomorphic Marketing'. *The Marketing Review* 10, no. 3 (2010): 209–224.

Cammaerts, B. 'Jamming the Political: Beyond Counter-hegemonic Practices'. *Continuum* 21, no. 1 (2007): 71–90.

Carducci, V. 'Culture Jamming: A Sociological Perspective'. *Journal of Consumer Culture* 6, no. 1 (2006): 116–138.

Chieng, Y. L., and C. L. Goi. 'Customer-based Brand Equity: A Study on Interrelationship among the Brand Equity Dimension in Malaysia'. *African Journal of Business Management* 5, no. 30 (2011): 11856.

Claudy, M. C., R. Garcia, and A. O'Driscoll. 'Consumer Resistance to Innovation: A Behavioral Reasoning Perspective'. *Journal of the Academy of Marketing Science* 43, no. 4 (2015): 528–544.

Cobb-Walgren, C. J., C. A. Ruble, and N. Donthu. 'Brand Equity, Brand Preference, and Purchase Intent'. *Journal of Advertising* 24, no. 3 (1995): 25–40.

Coulter, R. H., & Zaltman, G. *Using the Zaltman Metaphor Elicitation Technique to Understand Brand Images*. ACR North American Advances, 1994.

Coulter, R. H., and G. Zaltman. 'Seeing the Voice of the Customer: Metaphor-based Advertising Research'. *Journal of Advertising Research* 35, no. 4 (1995): 35.

David, A. *Building Strong Brands*. New York, NY: Free Press, 1996.

De Chernatony, L., and F. Dall'Olmo Riley. 'Defining a "Brand": Beyond the Literature with Experts' Interpretations'. *Journal of Marketing Management* 14, no. 5 (1998): 417–443.

DeLaure, M., M. Fink, and M. Dery, eds. *Culture Jamming: Activism and the Art of Cultural Resistance*. New York, NY: New York University Press, 2017.

Delgado-Ballester, E., and J. Luis Munuera-Alemán. 'Does Brand Trust Matter to Brand Equity? *Journal of Product & Brand Management* 14, no. 3 (2005): 187–196.

Dery, M. *Culture Jamming: Hacking, Slashing, and Sniping in the Empire of Signs* (Vol. 25). Westfield, NJ: Open Media, 1993.

De Sousa, R. L. 'Hitchcock's Queer Doubles'. Film-Philosophy Conference 2012, September.

Dobni, D., and G. M. Zinkhan. 'In Search of Brand Image: A Foundation Analysis'. In *NA-Advances in Consumer Research* (Vol. 17), edited by Marvin E. Goldberg, Gerald Gorn, and Richard W. Pollay, 110–119. Provo, UT: Association for Consumer Research, 1990.

Earle, Carey. 'FWD: This Made Me Laugh: How Viral Brand Parodies Impact Your Brand'. 2002. Available at: http://www.brandchannel.com/images/papers/FWD.pdf

Edelman, D. C. 'Branding in the Digital Age'. *Harvard Business Review* 88, no. 12 (2010): 62–69.

Enderwick, P., and S. Nagar. 'The Indian Premier League and Indian Cricket: Innovation in the Face of Tradition'. *Journal of Sponsorship* 3, no. 2 (2010): 130–143.

Fayrene, C. Y., and G. C. Lee. 'Customer-based Brand Equity: A Literature Review'. *Researchers World* 2, no. 1 (2011): 33.

Fishbein, M., and I. Ajzen. 'On Construct Validity: A Critique of Miniard and Cohen's Paper'. *Journal of Experimental Social Psychology* 17, no. 3 (1981): 340–350.

Fonseca, T. 'The Doppelgänger'. In *Icons of Horror and the Supernatural: An Encyclopedia of Our Worst Nightmares*

Troll Proof Branding in the Age of Doppelgangers

(Vol. 1), edited by S. T. Joshi, 187–214. Westport, CT: Greenwood Publishing Group, 2006.

Fournier, S., and J. Avery. 'The Uninvited Brand'. *Business Horizons* 54, no. 3 (2011): 193–207.

Freud, S. 'The Uncanny'. In *Fantastic Literature: A Critical Reader*, edited by David Sandner, 74–101. Westport, CT: Greenwood Publishing Group, 2004.

Freund, J., and E. S. Jacobi. 'Revenge of the Brand Monsters: How Goldman Sachs' Doppelgänger Turned Monstrous'. *Journal of Marketing Management* 29, no. 1–2 (2013): 175–194.

Füller, J., M. K. Lüdicke, and G. Jawecki. 'How Brands Enchant: Insights from Observing Community Driven Brand Creation'. *Advances in Consumer Research* 35 (2008): 359–366.

Gabl, S., V. E. Wieser, and A. Hemetsberger. 'Will We Hate Google One Day?' A Convention Theory Perspective on Public Brand Evaluations. *ACR North American Advances* (2016).

Giesler, M. 'How Doppelgänger Brand Images Influence the Market Creation Process: Longitudinal Insights from the Rise of Botox Cosmetic'. *Journal of Marketing* 76, no. 6 (2012): 55–68.

Gilson, E. 'Doppelgänger in Post-Wende Literature: Klaus Schlesinger's Trug and Beyond'. In *After the Wall: Remembering and Rethinking the GDR*, edited by Debbie Pinfold and Anna Saunders, 83–97. Basingstoke: Palgrave Macmillan, 2012.

Gladwell, M. *The Tipping Point: How Little Things Can Make a Big Difference*. Boston, MA: Little, Brown and Company, 2006.

Gobe, M. *Emotional Branding: The New Paradigm of Connecting Brands to People*. New York, NY: Allworth, 2001.

Grace, D., and A. O'Cass. 'Brand Associations: Looking through the Eye of the Beholder'. *Qualitative Market Research: An International Journal* 5, no. 2 (2002): 96–111.

Grime, I., A. Diamantopoulos, and G. Smith. 'Consumer Evaluations of Extensions and Their Effects on the Core Brand: Key Issues and Research Propositions'. *European Journal of Marketing* 36, no. 11/12 (2002): 1415–1438.

Guillory, J. 'Genesis of the Media Concept'. *Critical Inquiry* 36, no. 2 (2010): 321–362.

Gupta, A. 'Cricket: The Indianization of an Imperial Game'. In *The Oxford Handbook of Sports History*, edited by Robert Edelman and Wayne Wilson, 213. New York, NY: Oxford University Press, 2017.

Gupta, Amit. 'The IPL and the Indian Domination of Global Cricket'. *Sport in Society: Cultures, Commerce, Media, Politics* 14, no. 10 (2011): 1316–1325.

Gupta, A., A. Y. Naik, and N. Arora. 'Mapping Sponsorship-linked Marketing in Indian Premier League'. *IIM Kozhikode Society & Management Review* 2, no. 1 (2013): 61–72.

Guthrie, S. E. *Faces in the Clouds: A New Theory of Religion.* New York, NY: Oxford University Press, 1995.

Harold, C. 'Pranking Rhetoric: "Culture Jamming" as Media Activism'. *Critical Studies in Media Communication* 21, no. 3 (2004): 189–211.

Hearn, K., R. J. Mahncke, and P. A. Williams. 'Culture Jamming: From Activism to Hactivism. Australian Information Warfare and Security Conference, December 2009m p. 3.

Hoeffler, S., and K. L. Keller. 'The Marketing Advantages of Strong Brands'. *The Journal of Brand Management* 10, no. 6 (2003): 421–445.

Hogg, M. K. 'Anti-constellations: Exploring the Impact of Negation on consumption. *Journal of Marketing Management* 14, no. 1–3 (1998): 133–158.

Hollenbeck, C. R., and G. M. Zinkhan. 'Anti-brand Communities, Negotiation of Brand Meaning, and the Learning Process: The Case of Wal-Mart'. *Consumption, Markets and Culture* 13, no. 3 (2010): 325–345.

Lee, M. S., Motion, J., & Conroy, D. 'Anti-consumption and Brand Avoidance. *Journal of Business Research*, 62, no. 2 (2009): 169–180.

Holt, D. B. 'Why Do Brands Cause Trouble? A Dialectical Theory of Consumer Culture and Branding'. *Journal of Consumer Research* 29, no. 1 (2002): 70–90.

Holt, D., and D. Cameron. *Cultural Strategy: Using Innovative Ideologies to Build Breakthrough Brands*. New York, NY: Oxford University Press, 2010.

Hsieh, M. H. 'Identifying Brand Image Dimensionality and Measuring the Degree of Brand Globalization: A Cross-national Study'. *Journal of International Marketing* 10, no. 2 (2002): 46–67.

Iles III, D. M. 'The Contentious Performances of Culture Jamming: Art, Repertoires of Contention, and Social Movement Theory'. Doctoral diss., Louisiana State University, 2013.

Jalilvand, M. R., N. Samiei, and S. H. Mahdavinia. 'The Effect of Brand Equity Components on Purchase Intention: An Application of Aaker's Model in the Automobile Industry'. *International Business and Management* 2, no. 2 (2011): 149–158.

Jean, S. 'Brand Parody: A Communication Strategy to Attack a Competitor'. *Journal of Consumer Marketing* 28, no. 1 (2011): 19–26.

John, D. R., B. Loken, K. Kim, and A. B. Monga. 'Brand Concept Maps: A Methodology for Identifying Brand Association Networks'. *Journal of Marketing Research* 43, no. 4 (2006): 549–563.

Johnson, A. R., M. Matear, and M. Thomson. 'A Coal in the Heart: Self-relevance as a Post-exit Predictor of Consumer Anti-brand Actions'. *Journal of Consumer Research* 38, no. 1 (2011): 108–125.

Kadapa, S. S. 'How Sustainable Is the Strategy of the Indian Premier League-IPL? A Critical Review of 10 Key Issues That Impact the IPL Strategy'. *International Journal of Scientific and Research Publications* 3, no. 12 (2013). Available at: https://papers.ssrn.com/sol3/papers.cfm?abstract_id=2365587

Kapferer, J. N. *The New Strategic Brand Management: Advanced Insights and Strategic Thinking.* London: Kogan Page, 2012.

Kardes, F. R., M. L. Cronley, and T. W. Cline. *Consumer Behavior.* Mason, OH: South-Western Cengage Learning, 2011.

Kay, M. J. 'Strong Brands and Corporate Brands'. *European Journal of Marketing* 40, no. 7/8 (2006): 742–760.

Keller, K. L. 'Conceptualizing, Measuring, and Managing Customer-based Brand Equity'. *Journal of Marketing* 57, no. 1 (1993): 1–22.

Keller, K. L. 'Branding Perspectives on Social Marketing'. In *NA-Advances in Consumer Research* (Vol. 25), edited by Joseph W. Alba and J. Wesley Hutchinson. Provo, UT: Association for Consumer Research, 1998.

Keller, K. L. *Building Customer-based Brand Equity: A Blueprint for Creating Strong Brands,* 68–72. Cambridge, MA: Marketing Science Institute, 2001.

Keller, K. L. 'Brand Synthesis: The Multidimensionality of Brand Knowledge'. *Journal of Consumer Research* 29, no. 4 (2003): 595–600.

Keller, K. L. 'Understanding Brands, Branding and Brand Equity'. *Interactive Marketing* 5, no. 1 (2003): 7–20.

Klein, N. 'Culture Jamming: Ads under Attack'. *Brandweek* 41, no. 28 (2000): 28–35.

Klein, N., and B. Byam. *No Logo: Taking Aim at the Brand Bullies*, 1328–1330. Ontario: Canadian National Institute for the Blind, 2000.

Kotler, P. *Marketing Management* (Millennium Edition), Custom Edition for University of Phoenix, 9. Hoboken, NJ: Prentice Hall, 2000.

Kozinets, R. V., and J. M. Handelman. 'Adversaries of Consumption: Consumer Movements, Activism, and Ideology'. *Journal of Consumer Research* 31, no. 3 (2004): 691–704.

Krishnamurthy, S., and S. U. Kucuk. 'Anti-branding on the Internet'. *Journal of Business Research* 62, no. 11 (2009): 1119–1126.

Kucuk, S. U. 'Negative Double Jeopardy: The Role of Anti-brand Sites on the Internet'. *Journal of Brand Management* 15, no. 3 (2008): 209–222.

Kucuk, S. U. 'What Is Brand Hate?' In *Brand Hate*, 17–36. New York, NY: Springer International Publishing, 2016.

Kucuk, S. U. 'Consequences of Brand Hate'. In *Brand Hate*, 57–66. New York, NY: Springer International Publishing, 2016.

Kucuk, S. U. 'Managing Brand Hate'. In *Brand Hate*, 125–136. New York, NY: Springer International Publishing, 2016.

Kucuk, S. U. 'What Is Hate?' In *Brand Hate*, 1–15). New York, NY: Springer International Publishing, 2016.

Kuhn, K. A. L., Alpert, F., and Pope, N. K. L. 'An Application of Keller's Brand Equity Model in a B2B Context'. *Qualitative Market Research: An International Journal* 11, no. 1 (2008): 40–58.

Lakshman, C., and M. Akhter. 'Corporate Governance Scandals in the Indian Premier League (IPL): Implications for Labour'. *Labour & Industry: A Journal of the Social and Economic Relations of Work* 23, no. 1 (2013): 89–106.

Lassar, W., B. Mittal, and A. Sharma. 'Measuring Customer-based Brand Equity'. *Journal of Consumer Marketing* 12, no. 4 (1995): 11–19.

Lee, M. S., J. Motion, and D. Conroy. 'Anti-consumption and Brand Avoidance'. *Journal of Business Research* 62, no, 2 (2009): 169–180.

Lee, Z., J. McCloskey, and M. Beverland. '"It'S a Bit of a Mask, It'S Not Pure... It'S Not What I Thought": How Doppelgänger Brand Images Attack Brand Authenticity'. In *ACR Asia-Pacific Advances* (Vol. 11), edited by Echo Wen Wan and Meng Zhang, 173–174. Duluth, MN: Association for Consumer Research, 2015.

Low, G. S., and C. W. Lamb Jr. 'The Measurement and Dimensionality of Brand Associations'. *Journal of Product & Brand Management* 9, no. 6 (2000): 350–370.

Luedicke, M. K., and M. Giesler. 'Contested Consumption in Everyday Life'. In *ACR North American Advances* (Vol. 35), edited by Angela Y. Lee and Dilip Soman, 812–813. Duluth, MN: Association for Consumer Research, 2008.

Luedicke, M. K., C. J. Thompson, and M. Giesler. 'Consumer Identity Work as Moral Protagonism: How Myth and Ideology Animate a Brand-mediated Moral

Conflict'. *Journal of Consumer Research* 36, no. 6 (2009): 1016–1032.

McCaughey, M., and M. D. Ayers, eds. *Cyberactivism: Online Activism in Theory and Practice*. Oxfordshire: Routledge, 2013.

Mehrabian, A. *Silent Messages* (Vol. 8). Belmont, CA: Wadsworth, 1971.

Menon, V. P., and G. Barani. 'Dimensions of Brand Equity: An Investigation on Higher Education Institutions'. *Asian Journal of Research in Social Sciences and Humanities* 6, no. 5 (2016): 353–359.

Micali, S. 'The Hero and His Shadow'. *Image & Narrative* 11, no. 3 (2010): 99–110.

Milstein, T., and A. Pulos. 'Culture Jam Pedagogy and Practice: Relocating Culture by Staying on One's Toes'. *Communication, Culture & Critique* 8, no. 3 (2015): 395–413.

Misra, B. B. *The Indian Middle Classes: Their Growth in Modern Times*. Bombay: Oxford University Press, 1963.

O'Meara, A., J. Davies, and S. Hammond. 'The Psychometric Properties and Utility of the Short Sadistic Impulse Scale (SSIS)'. *Psychological Assessment* 23, no. 2 (2011): 523.

Østergaard, P., J. Hermansen, and J. Fitchett. 'Structures of Brand and Anti-brand Meaning: A Semiotic Square Analysis of Reflexive Consumption'. *The Journal of Brand Management* 22, no. 1 (2015): 60–77.

Parker, D., P. Burns, and H. Natarajan. 'Player Valuations in the Indian Premier League'. *Frontier Economics* (October 2008): 1–16.

Parmentier, M. A., and E. Fischer. 'Things Fall Apart: The Dynamics of Brand Audience Dissipation'. *Journal of Consumer Research* 41, no. 5 (2014): 1228–1251.

Peretti, J., and M. Micheletti. 'The Nike Sweatshop Email: Political Consumerism, Internet, and Culture Jamming'. In *Politics, Products, and Markets. Exploring Political Consumerism Past and Present*, edited by Michele Micheletti, Andreas Follesdal, and Dietlind Stolle, 127–142. New Brunswick, NJ: Transaction Publishers, 2011.

Pfeffer, J., T. Zorbach, and K. M. Carley. 'Understanding Online Firestorms: Negative Word-of-Mouth Dynamics in Social Media Networks'. *Journal of Marketing Communications* 20, no. 1–2 (2014): 117–128.

Radford, B. *Bad Clowns*. Albuquerque, NM: UNM Press, 2016.

Reder, L. M., and J. R. Anderson. 'A Partial Resolution of the Paradox of Interference: The Role of Integrating Knowledge'. *Cognitive Psychology* 12, no. 4 (1980): 447–472.

Ries, A., and J. Trout. *Positioning: The Battle for Your Mind*. New York, NY: McGraw-Hill, 1981.

Romani, S., S. Grappi, L. Zarantonello, and R. P. Bagozzi. 'The Revenge of the Consumer! How Brand Moral Violations Lead to Consumer Anti-brand Activism'. *The Journal of Brand Management* 22, no. 8 (2015): 658–672.

Roth, M. S. 'The Effects of Culture and Socioeconomics on the Performance of Global Brand Image Strategies'. *Journal of Marketing Research* 32, no. 2 (1995): 163–175.

Rowley, J., and D. Edmundson-Bird. 'Brand Presence in Digital Space'. *Journal of Electronic Commerce in Organizations* 11, no. 1 (2013): 63–78.

Saikia, H., D. Bhattacharjee, and A. Bhattacharjee. 'Is IPL Responsible for Cricketers' Performance in Twenty20 World Cup'. *International Journal of Sports Science and Engineering* 6, no. 2 (2012): 96–110.

Sandlin, J. A. 'Popular Culture, Cultural Resistance, and Anticonsumption Activism: An Exploration of Culture Jamming as Critical Adult Education'. *New Directions for*

Adult and Continuing Education 2007, no. 115 (2007): 73–82.

Schneider, S. 'Monsters as (Uncanny) Metaphors: Freud, Lakoff, and the Representation of Monstrosity in Cinematic Horror'. *Other Voices* 1, no. 3 (1999).

Schnittka, O., H. Sattler, and S. Zenker. 'Advanced Brand Concept Maps: A New Approach for Evaluating the Favorability of Brand Association Networks'. *International Journal of Research in Marketing* 29, no. 3 (2012): 265–274.

Sengupta, S. *Brand Positioning.* New Delhi: Tata McGraw-Hill Publishing Company, 1990.

Shin, J. 'Morality and Internet Behavior: A Study of the Internet Troll and Its Relation with Morality on the Internet'. Society for Information Technology & Teacher Education International Conference, 2834–2840. Association for the Advancement of Computing in Education (AACE), March 2008.

Sivitanides, M., and V. Shah. 'The Era of Digital Activism'. Conference for Information Systems Applied Research (Vol. 4), 1–8, 2011.

Sood, G., and J. K. Sharma. 'A Historical Background to Genesis of Brand Doppelgänger'. *American International Journal of Research in Humanities, Arts and Social Sciences* 16, no. 3, September–November (2016): 201–206.

Sood, Gaurav, and J. K. Sharma. The IPL Brandenstein – Creation of a Monstrous Doppelgänger Imagery, *American International Journal of Research in Humanities, Arts and Social Sciences* 12, no. 2, September–November (2015): 241–245.

Sood, Gaurav, and J. K. Sharma. 'An Empirical Research into IPLs Brand Doppelgänger'. *International Journal of Public Sector Performance Management.* doi:10.1504/IJPSPM.2021.10039726

Stevenson, R. L. *The Strange Case of Dr. Jekyll and Mr. Hyde* (Vol. 1). Alexandria: Library of Alexandria, 1927.

Suler, J. 'The Online Disinhibition Effect'. *Cyberpsychology & Behavior* 7, no. 3 (2004): 321–326.

Thompson, C. J., A. Rindfleisch, and Z. Arsel. 'Emotional Branding and the Strategic Value of the Doppelgänger Brand Image'. *Journal of Marketing* 70, no. 1 (2006), 50–64.

Trammell III, T. I. *Fake News Risk: Modeling Management Decisions to Combat Disinformation.* Stanford: Stanford University, 2020.

Travis, D. 'Branding in the Digital Age'. *Journal of Business Strategy* 22, no. 3 (2001): 14–18.

Trout, J. '"Positioning" Is a Game People Play in Today's Me-too Market Place'. *Industrial Marketing* 54, no. 6 (June 1969): 51–55.

Van den Bergh, J., and M. Behrer. *How Cool Brands Stay Hot: Branding to Generations Y and Z.* London: Kogan Page, 2016.

Vardoulakis, D. 'The Return of Negation: The Doppelgänger in Freud's "The Uncanny"'. *SubStance* 35, no. 2 (2006): 100–116.

Watkins, B. 'An Integrated Approach to Sports Branding: Examining the Influence of Social Media on Brand Outcomes'. *International Journal of Integrated Marketing Communications* 6, no. 2 (2014): 30–40.

Webber, A. J. *The Doppelgänger: Double Visions in German Literature.* Oxford: Clarendon Press, 1996.

Wood, L. 'Brands and Brand Equity: Definition and Management'. *Management Decision* 38, no. 9 (2000): 662–669.

Yoo, B., N. Donthu, and S. Lee. 'An Examination of Selected Marketing Mix Elements and Brand Equity'. *Journal of the Academy of Marketing Science* 28, no. 2 (2000): 195–211.

Zaltman, G. 'Rethinking Market Research: Putting People Back in'. *Journal of Marketing Research* 34, no. 4 (1997): 424–437.

Zaltman, Gerald. *How Customers Think: Essential Insights into the Mind of the Market*. Boston, MA: Harvard Business Review Press, 2003.

Živković, M. 'The Double as the "Unseen" of Culture: Toward a Definition of Doppelgänger'. *Facta Universitatis- Linguistics and Literature* 2, no. 7 (2000): 121–128.

ABOUT THE AUTHOR

Professor (Dr) Gaurav Sood is a brand evangelist, researcher, educator, speaker, columnist and author, with more than two-decade practice creating strong brands. He has been an integral part of developing and managing marketing and integrated marketing communication campaigns for global brands in India, Germany and the United States. He has carved out a niche as a brand strategist and pioneer in the domain of brand research.

He has seen the evolving face of global media and advertising and contributed immensely towards rejuvenating and lending a fresh perspective towards brand communication to major corporate players in the realms of engineering, IT, telecommunications, FMCG, services, consumer durables and media marketing—in both in India and the United States.

He is Professor of Marketing at Amity School of Business, Amity University, India. His research work has focused on the nouveau field of 'doppelganger brand imagery', and his research papers and articles have been published in leading academic journals and business and marketing magazines. His work has also achieved remarkable acceptance by academicians and practitioners across multiple fields. He has also authored four books:

1. *Impact of Doppelganger Brand Image on Indian Premiere League (IPL)*—2018

2. *Global Business Strategies for Sustainability*—2019, co-edited by Gaurav Sood and J. K. Sharma

3. *Global Business Strategies for Sustainability*—2021, co-edited by Gaurav Sood and J. K. Sharma

4. *Troll Proof Branding in the Age of Doppelganger*—2022

He is an alumnus of Amity University (PhD); Emerson College, Boston; Institute of Management Technology, Ghaziabad; and Panjab University, Chandigarh. He keeps his own website www.gauravsood.in. He is a notable guest blogger at BW Businessworld.

Dr Sood is also on the editorial board of reputed international journals such as *International Journal on Document Analysis and Recognition* (IJDAR) and *International Journal of Public Sector Performance Management.*

STAY **ENCOURAGED**
STAY **CREATIVE**
STAY **MOTIVATED**

Keep abreast of the most cutting-edge thinking driving businesses today.

www.sagepub.in